DATE DUE

Vegetarian Soup
Cuisine

Other Books by Jay Solomon

Vegetarian Rice Cuisine

Lean Bean Cuisine

*The Global Vegetarian: Adventures
in a Meatless Kitchen*

A Taste of the Tropics

Global Grilling

Chutneys, Relishes, and Table Sauces

Vegetarian Soup Cuisine

125 Soups and Stews from Around the World

Jay Solomon

PRIMA PUBLISHING

Prima Publishing and colophon are trademarks of Prima Communications, Inc.

Cover design by The Dunlavey Studio, Inc.

Library of Congress Cataloging-in-Publication Data
Solomon, Jay.
    Vegetarian soup cuisine : 125 savory soups and hearty stews from around the world / by Jay Solomon.
      p.   cm.
    Includes index.
    ISBN 0-7615-0190-8
    1. Soups. 2. Stews. 3. Vegetarian cookery. 4. Cookery, International.
  I. Title.
TX757.S633   1995   95-36299
641.8'313—dc20   CIP

95 96 97 98 99 DD 10 9 8 7 6 5 4 3 2 1
Printed in the United States of America.

How to Order:

Single copies may be ordered from Prima Publishing, P.O. Box 1260BK, Rocklin, CA 95677; telephone (916) 632-4400. Quantity discounts are also available. On your letterhead, include information concerning the intended use of the books and the number of books you wish to purchase.

This book is dedicated to two of my good friends,
Jessica Robin and Shaun Buckley,
whose wit and humor have sustained well more
than one bowl of soup over the years.

Contents

Chapter 5   Savory Soups in the Springtime   156

Contents   *ix*

Chapter 6   Summer Bowls and Fruity Bisques   204

Chapter 7   Soup Garnishes and Accompaniments   236

Index   259

About the Author   267

Acknowledgments

For years I have wanted to write a soup cookbook. With *Vegetarian Soup Cuisine*, my long time aspiration has been realized. I would like to thank Georgia Hughes, Acquisitions Editor at Prima Publishing, for endorsing and encouraging this deeply rooted culinary ambition.

I would like to thank many of my friends who savored and sipped numerous bowls of soup along the way: Emily Robin, Marilee and Eamonn Murphy, Jessica Robin, Gaby Robin, Sarah Huber, Helena Das, Beth Ryan, Tammy Palmer, Jeannette McGrogan, and Linda and Jon Meyerhoff.

I would also like to acknowledge distant friends who have offered plenty of ideas: Robert and Amy Cima, Shaun Buckley, Janet Welch, Leslie Sadoff, Freddi Pollack, and the Robin Family from Chappaqua, New York. My immediate and extended family have been more than generous with their sagacious thoughts: Jesse and Ann Solomon, Greg Solomon, Lisa Solomon, Margaret Shalaby, Dick and Margaret Solomon, Robert Caliel, and my grandmother, Mary Badia.

I would also like to thank the Healthy Heart Agency of Tompkins County, the School of Hotel Administration at Cornell University, and the local Cornell Cooperative Extension for providing valuable background information and assistance for this book.

Vegetarian Soup Cuisine

Introduction

A savory, steaming bowl of soup brings pleasure to the palate, nourishment to the body, and comfort to the soul. Simmering soup on the stove top fills the kitchen with warm and enticing aromas. When the soup's on, all is well. Soup is welcome therapy for the body and the spirit.

Vegetarian Soup Cuisine features a plethora of appetizing and nourishing soups, stews, chowders, and bisques. This new world of soup cookery exudes healthful, vibrant flavors; inviting textures; bold colors; and fragrant scents. In this meatless brand of soup cookery, cauldrons are filled with garden vegetables, refreshing herbs, and assertive spices. A surfeit of grains, pastas, and beans stock the pot and provide lasting satisfaction and sustenance.

In *Vegetarian Soup Cuisine,* there are soup meals for every season and occasion throughout the year. In A Harvest of Autumn Soups and Stews, a cornucopia of high-spirited tureens are sure to pique one's palate: Curried Squash and Autumn Greens Soup; Sweet Potato and Leek Bisque, Succotash Squash Soup; and Tarragon Carrot Bisque are some of the autumnal bowls of plenty.

As the days grow shorter, the variety of soups grows longer and more abundant. In Winter Rhapsodies: Every Day a Soup Day, an array of enticing soup meals promises to slay the hungry appetite. From Sizzling Black Bean Soup, Split Pea and Wild Rice Soup, and Mondo Chili to Tuscan Country Bean and Escarole Soup, Beet Gumbo, Root Vegetable Pot au Feu, and myriad others, these soups will sate and satisfy while banishing the winter chill.

With the warming of spring comes Savory Soups in the Springtime, a selection of inventive and inspiring seasonal soups such as Minestrone with Arugula Pesto, Champagne Mushroom Soup, Artichoke and White Bean Stew, Emily's Asparagus Vichyssoise, and others. These lean tureens offer the lively, salubrious flavors ideal for both April showers and May flowers.

Soup is more than an antidote for cold weather blues; in Summery Bowls and Fruity Bisques, light and healthful recipes offer welcome shade for the sun-wilted palate. Couscous Gazpacho, Key West Sunset Avocado Bisque, A Master Gardener's Country Stew, and Grilled and Chilled Vegetable Soup are some of the alluring soup meals perfect for summertime dining. For before (or after) meals, fruity Peach Orchard Soup, Cherry Apricot Bisque, and Minty Cantaloupe Bisque provide cool relief and replenishment.

Finally, there are Soup Garnishes and Accompaniments, a compendium of soup-friendly accompaniments ranging from Chipotle Cornbread, Yellow Squash Muffins, and Pumpkin Currant Scones to Poblano Rouille and Herb Forest Pesto. These flavorful embellishments serve to enhance and heighten the overall soup dining experience.

Soup is versatile as well as multiseasonal. When served as a first course, soup stimulates and whets the palate for the meal to come. When accompanied with a loaf of crusty bread and salad of leafy greens, a light soup meal is born. When the kettle is filled with vegetables, beans, and grains or pastas, a bountiful soup supper is bound to ensue. Soup can even appear at meal's end; cool fruity bisques provide a flourish at the finish.

The recipes in *Vegetarian Soup Cuisine* strive to be healthful, nutritious, and rich in seasonal vegetables, grains, pastas, beans, and leafy greens. Herbs and spices are often called upon to enliven and invigorate the pot: fresh garlic is ubiquitous and indispensable, and chile peppers offer exuberant, piquant flavors. This enlightened (and liberated) approach to soup cookery is entirely free of any meat, cream, butter, commercial bouillon cubes, bases, or canned stocks.

Soup making is a most forgiving craft. Motley, odd lot, humble vegetables are transformed and elevated into sophisticated gourmet creations. Advanced culinary knowledge is not required (though always welcome) nor is there a need for trendy kitchen gadgets. What matters is an appreciation of taste and aesthetics, a sense of time, and a willingness (on occasion) to explore adventurous culinary terrain.

For centuries, soups, stews, and chowders have simmered and steeped on stove tops throughout the world. Soup meals have been universally cherished in almost every culture and climate: there's Italian *zuppa*, Portuguese *caldo*, Spanish and Mexican *sopa*, French *potage*, and on and on. In *Vegetarian Soup Cuisine*, the art of soup cookery enters another era, one redolent with bold, worldly flavors, striking combinations, and good-for-you staples.

As a longtime restaurant owner, chef, and soup connoisseur, I have prepared a plethora of soups, stews, bisques, and chilies on a daily basis. While traveling throughout the land I have sipped, slurped, and gulped my way through a multitude of bowls in a search of new and intriguing fare. Over the years I have simmered and stirred huge cauldrons of soup for two hundred and fifty people; I have gathered with friends for intimate supper buffets of eclectic soups, homemade breads, and winsome wines; and more than once I have found inner calm and relief while savoring a bowl of soup in quiet solitude.

Vegetarian Soup Cuisine chronicles the many soups, stews, and chowders I have simmered, nurtured, and savored over my lifetime. I invite you to join in the immense pleasures and rewards of this new soup cookery.

Soup's on!

Jay Solomon

Ithaca, New York

Chapter 1

The Art of
Soup Cookery

Soup cookery is the most democratic of kitchen endeavors. Anyone can make a delicious soup, from the beginning cook to the aspiring chef. If you can bring water to a boil and follow a recipe, the world of soups is within your grasp. There are no barriers, no clubs to join, no complicated culinary techniques to master. In the realm of soup cookery, everyone is invited. Welcome aboard.

The recipes in *Vegetarian Soup Cuisine* are the guidelines for creating exciting and pleasurable soup meals. On your path to preparing delicious soups, let these recipes be the points of your compass and steer you in the right direction. However, there is plenty of room for improvisation and personal taste—by all means you are encouraged to unleash the creativity within.

Stocking the soup kitchen is easy. In addition to the usual kitchen tools—knives, peelers, colanders, cutting boards, and so forth—all you need is a large sturdy pot, a stirring spoon, and a soup ladle. A blender or food processor is a prerequisite for creating pureed bisques. All in all, there is little need for the latest kitchen techno-gadgets.

Just as adventurous journeys begin with a map, the new soup cuisine follows along a sequence of steps. Here is an overview of the life of a soup or stew, from stove top to tabletop.

Pillars of Flavor: Sautéed Vegetables

Soup begins with an aromatic base of sautéed vegetables. This mixture, such as onion, celery, bell peppers, and garlic, is briefly cooked in a small amount of oil over high heat. The initial sautéing sears and seals in the flavors while releasing a natural caramelized essence. It is a universal step; Italians call it *soffritto;* in French, it is *mirepoix;* and in Spanish, *sofrito.* Whatever the term, the aromatic base forms a flavorful foundation for the well-cooked soup.

The mixture of sautéed vegetables varies from soup to stew. Gumbos include a venerated trio of onion, bell pepper, and celery (Cajuns call them the "holy trinity"). A minestrone might start with onion, zucchini, celery, and garlic. A Southwestern stew would likely include bell peppers, onion, garlic, and chile peppers. A curried pumpkin bisque might begin with onions, ginger, carrots, and tomatoes.

Throughout *Vegetarian Soup Cuisine,* most recipes call for vegetables to be sautéed together in a little canola oil or pure olive oil, which are both low in saturated fats. Cooks on a restricted lowfat diet may use a mixture of oil and white wine (or all wine) or vegetable spray; the choice is up to you. However, butter or margarine are never called for.

Body and Soul: Adding Liquids, Hearty Vegetables, and Starches

After the vegetables are sautéed, either water or vegetable stock is poured in. The liquid supplies the soup with necessary body and allows the flavors to expand and mingle. Although vegetable stocks provide essential flavors and nutrients, it is important to note that water will suffice for most long-simmering soups, which in effect create their own stock (or broth) in the process.

After the liquid come the starches—hearty vegetables and winter squash, such as potatoes, butternut squash, carrots, root vegetables, and sweet potatoes. These ingredients form the infrastructure of the soup by adding substance, body, nutrients, and textures. The vegetables endow the soup with character; they give you something to sink your teeth into as well.

Grains, pastas, and rices are also added to the pot during this phase. To avoid overcooking pastas and grains, it is best to add them near the middle or end of the cooking time; white long grain rice cooks in about twenty minutes and pasta cooks in ten to twelve minutes. When the grains or pasta are tender and done cooking (al dente), the soup should also be done. Overcooking risks bloating the soup. Whole grains take longer to cook—from forty minutes to one hour—and can be added much earlier in the cooking process.

Long-cooking beans, split peas, and lentils are often added at the beginning of the soup along with the liquid. Legumes may also be cooked separately and added to the *sofrito* with their cooking liquid—in this way the beans' cooking liquid doubles as a soup's broth. Canned beans should be added near the end of the soup's simmering phase, since they only need to be reheated.

Flavor Fusions with Herbs and Spices

Spicing is another crucial element in the life of a well-made soup. Herbs and spices help the soup develop a distinctive personality and flavor dimensions. From oregano, thyme, basil, and parsley to cumin, curry, paprika, and ground peppers, a battery of herbs and spices enhances and enlightens a variety of soups and stews. Dried herbs and spices are typically added along with the liquid.

We are in the midst of a spicing revolution; more spices are sold and used today than ever before. The dull, bland days of yesteryear are becoming a distant memory (thankfully). By incorporating a variety of seasonings in your repertoire (and spice rack), you'll expand the range of flavors within your reach. As an added health bonus, well-balanced spicing also reduces the need for salt. So spice it up!

Simmering, Steeping, and Stirring

As the soup simmers and steeps, an aroma fills the kitchen, and a kind of culinary transformation takes place. Potatoes, squash, and carrots become tender and enrich the broth. Garlic, dried herbs, and spices infuse the liquid with their aromatic presence. As the broth develops fluidity and flavor, it becomes what the French call *bouillon,* Italians call *brodo,* and my grandmother calls *zoom.*

During this time it is important to *occasionally* stir the kettle. Stirring coaxes and cajoles the ingredients to meld and mingle; as a practical matter, stirring keeps ingredients from sticking to the bottom and burning. Simmer the soup or stew on low or medium-low heat for the duration; any higher runs the risk of uneven cooking, scorched bottoms, and the ruination of your masterpiece. Perfection cannot be rushed.

Lowfat Thickeners

Many of the soups and stews in *Vegetarian Soup Cuisine* contain lowfat, nutritious thickeners. In this new world of soup cookery, there is little need for artery-clogging heavy cream or buttery roux, the traditional thickeners of soups past. A well-made soup thickens as it simmers.

For instance, well-cooked potatoes, root vegetables, and winter squash, when mashed against the side of the pan or pureed afterward, function as natural thickeners. Grains, beans, and pastas add substance to the broth as they cook and expand. Pureeing a small portion of a soup and returning it to the pan is another way to produce thick, dense soups and stews with fluidity.

Tomato paste and crushed tomatoes make excellent thickeners for tomato-based soups. For Asian-style soups, a slurry mixture of cornstarch and water does the trick. Dumplings also indirectly add body to soups and stews.

Secret Touches and Last-Minute Garnishes

When the soup is heading down the final stretch, it is a golden opportunity to perk up the pot with down-to-the-wire infusions of flavor. With a sense for taste and an eye for presentation, there are a variety of healthful, lowfat, low-sodium ways to rev up and revive a soup and imbue the cauldron with alluring flavors.

For starters, fresh garden herbs bring instant vitality to almost any soup or stew. Parsley, basil, arugula, chives, watercress, and other flavorful herbs add spritely flavors and bright colors to the soup pot. Unlike dried herbs, which come in near the beginning, fresh herbs are best added near the end; long cooking deprives them of their vivid flavors. For example, cilantro adds zest to spicy soups; basil and oregano enhance tomato-based soups; thyme enhances chowders; and ubiquitous parsley is welcome in almost any soup or stew.

This is also the time for adding light acidic touches, such as a squeeze of lemon or a few drops of vinegar. These simple flavor enhancers do wonders for bland or flat-tasting soups in need of a tighter focus. Vichyssoise, borscht, potato bisques, lowfat dairy soups, and low-sodium soups benefit from a smidgen of tartness. Also, a twist of fresh ground black pepper adds a warm tingle at the table. Chopped crisp scallions make a colorful green garnish when sprinkled over the top just before serving.

There are a variety of chopped leafy greens that can join the soup pot for the last five or ten minutes of cooking. Kale, Swiss chard, escarole, turnip greens, spinach, and other seasonal leafy greens bring valuable nutrients and striking flavors to soup cookery. Simply coarsely chop the leaves (or cut chiffonade style: rolled up and cut into ribbons) and stir in the pot.

It is a good idea to serve hot soups in warm bowls and chilled soups in cold bowls. Another thought: Do not shy away from making a large batch of soup since it will improve with age (up to a point, of course). Most soups can be prepared days ahead of time, refrigerated, and reheated upon demand. The ingredients and the broth marinate, marry, and meld together.

Bread and Soup: Natural Companions

An in-depth discussion about soup would be woefully incomplete without mentioning bread, soup's natural table companion. Bread soaks up precious broth, provides sustenance, and allows one to wipe the bowl clean with gustatory vigor.

In general, choose whole-grain, firm-textured breads with a sound constitution. Dark breads go well with beet soups, bean soups, and chowders; Italian breads sop up tomato, pasta, and bean soups; French bread is amenable to almost any soup (especially brothy soups and chowders); and cheese breads complement spicy soups and chili. It is important to avoid at all cost the flimsy, mushy, wimpy white breads, most of which are devoid of any nutrients or character.

Soup cuisine is not limited to loaf-style breads. There are a host of ethnic breads that make appealing soup partners. Pita bread scoops up thick lentil soups and Middle Eastern soups; flour tortillas complement bean soups and Mexican chowders; and Indian flat breads (nan, chapati, and roti) accompany curry soups and spicy Caribbean cauldrons. Corn bread makes a fitting companion for gumbo, chili, and *posole*.

Almost any fresh-baked bread can accompany almost any soup at the table. The sight of a hunk of bread and bowl of soup resting on the table is a thing of beauty and is bound to fill the room with anticipation.

A Short Digression about Soup Stocks

Today's high-flavored vegetarian cookery does not depend on stocks—liquids which have historically contained meat, poultry, or fish. For the recipes in *Vegetarian Soup Cuisine,* it is more important to have a well-stocked spice cabinet, access to fresh garlic, garden herbs, and chile peppers, and an appreciation of the myriad vegetables available to the modern cook. This seasoning philosophy, when combined with vegetable stock or plain water, has made meat-laden broths obsolete within these pages.

Vegetable stocks are easy and economical to make. Simply coarsely chop a variety of vegetables and herbs, place them in a large sturdy pot, and cover with water. Bring the pot to a simmer and cook for about one hour over low heat. Afterward, let the mixture cool slightly and then strain the vegetable pulp, saving the enriched liquid. The vegetable broth should have an aromatic and tealike flavor.

You don't have to use your best vegetables for the stock; rather, include leftover vegetables (not rotten, of course, but specimens slightly past their prime). Save your trimmings for stock, such as onion skins, wilted carrots and carrot peels, celery ends, broccoli stalks, bell pepper ribs, kale or Swiss chard stems, herb branches, and other remnants. Collect your trimmings in the freezer until you can fill a whole pot, then proceed with the stock recipe.

As mentioned earlier, water will suffice for many recipes. A long-simmering soup filled with vegetables, herbs, spices, and water essentially creates its own stock. There are several other creative ways to enhance a soup. For example, save the cooking broth from beans or lentils, or the water from blanched or steamed broccoli, asparagus, peas, corn, and other vegetables. If you have an abundance of fresh herbs, they too can be simmered for thirty minutes and strained. So there are many options, none of which requires meat or store-bought canned stocks and bases.

The trouble with canned chicken and beef stocks, bouillon cubes, and meat and poultry bases lies in their hidden sodium, fat, sugar, monosodium glutamate, and other unhealthy additives. Additionally, soups containing canned stocks or bouillon cubes all begin to taste alike. Eventually, the taste buds are numbed by the monotonous flavors. These commercial preparations are a convenient refuge for the undiscerning palate or harried cook, but in vegetarian soup cookery, they should be relegated to the dustbin of history.

Versatile Vegetable Stock

Here is a basic recipe, but feel free to improvise. If there are leftover parsnips, tomatoes, or stems from leafy greens, add those as well. If you desire a piquant broth, add a few chile peppers. Ginger adds a fragrant nuance; beets turn the broth magenta. Experiment on your own, and remember, variety is the spice of life.

3	to 4 carrots, washed and coarsely chopped
2	red or green bell peppers, coarsely chopped
2	large yellow onions, coarsely chopped
3	or 4 celery stalks and leaves, coarsely chopped
4	to 6 whole garlic cloves
1	bunch broccoli, coarsely chopped
1	small bunch parsley, stems and all, chopped
	About 6 cups water (to cover)
1/4	cup dry white or red wine (optional)

Combine all of the ingredients in a large stockpot; the vegetables should be barely covered with water. Bring to a simmer and cook for about 1 hour over low heat. If necessary, add more water to keep the vegetables immersed.

Strain the vegetables and save the liquid. Discard the vegetables and use the liquid for soups and stews. If kept refrigerated, the stock should last for 5 to 7 days.

Yield: About 4 cups

Chapter 2

The International Soup Pantry

Today's soup pantry includes a cornucopia of seasonal vegetables, tubers, roots, leafy greens, herbs, grains, legumes, pastas, and spices. Here are the most frequently used ingredients in the new soup cuisine.

Garden Herbs

Fresh herbs perk up simmering soups and stews with lively, enlightening flavors. At the same time, herbs decrease the need for salt or cream. Remember to add the herbs near the end of the cooking time, since most fresh herbs lose their potency if cooked in the pot for too long. (Thyme is an exception—it benefits from a long steeping time.)

Arugula: Also called rocket or roquette, this oak-shaped narrow green leaf has a peppery zip to it. The larger the leaf, the more pronounced the flavor. Arugula complements basil in Italian tomato-based soups and also matches well with cilantro in bean soups and leafy green bisques.

Basil: The queen of herbs has a spirited, cleansing flavor with hints of anise and mint. Best known as the herb in pesto, basil enhances tomato-based soups, chowders, bean soups, and Thai soups. Varieties include Thai basil, opal (purple) basil, sweet basil, lemon basil, and ruffled basil.

Cilantro: Although similar to flat-leaf parsley in appearance, cilantro has a pungent, palate-awaking taste. Also known as Chinese parsley and coriander, the herb is prevalent in Indian, Mexican, Caribbean, and African soups. Cilantro's dried seeds are called coriander.

Marjoram: This tender greenish blue petal is very similar to oregano. It has a smart, resinlike flavor and is interchangeable with oregano. Marjoram complements basil and arugula quite well.

Mint: There is a wide variety of mint to choose from, including apple, pineapple, orange, spearmint, and peppermint. Mint adds clean, refreshing flavors to chilled fruit soups and cold vegetable soups such as gazpacho.

Oregano: This small, oval petal is one of the few herbs that is stronger when dried. Oregano has a resinous flavor similar to marjoram and makes a natural companion to basil.

Parsley: This versatile herb brings a welcome aftertaste to almost any soup or stew. There are two varieties: the common curly leaf and the slightly stronger flat leaf, also called Italian parsley. Parsley is widely available all year round.

Thyme: This herb has a strong, pungent scent that belies its tiny oval leaves. Thyme retains most of its flavor during the cooking process and is great in chowders, bean soups, and squash bisques. Common thyme is the most popular, but there are also lemon thyme, pineapple thyme, creeping thyme, and others.

Watercress: These round, delicate leaves add a tangy, sometimes peppery flavor to soups and stews. Watercress is a popular garnish for Asian soups, gazpacho, and chowders.

Aromatics: Garlic, Ginger, and Lemon Grass

Garlic: This potent bulbous herb is cherished all over the world. Peeled and chopped, garlic brings a redolent presence to a multitude of soups and stews. There is no substitute for fresh garlic—not garlic powder, garlic salt, nor tinny crushed garlic.

Ginger Root: This knobby, gnarly tan root has a clean, sharp lemony essence. Once minced, ginger can be added to curry soups and often shows up in African, Asian, Caribbean, and Indian soups. Dried ground ginger is not a substitute.

Lemon Grass: This brittle, pale green herbal stalk is prominent in light Asian soups. Peel the outer sheaf and finely chop the inner core. Lemon grass has a faint lemon-lime scent.

Chile Peppers

A variety of chile peppers infuse soups and stews with pungent, penetrating nuances. Chiles also contain vitamins A and C and other nutrients, and are low in fat and sodium. In addition, their assertive presence diminishes the need for salty or buttery flavors in the pot.

Here are few preparation tips: After cutting off the stem, slit the chile pod in half lengthwise. Slide a butter knife along the inside of the pepper and remove the seeds. Now the pepper can be minced or chopped. It is a good idea to wear plastic or rubber gloves when handling the peppers, since their heat may irritate your skin.

Chiles can be roasted over a hot grill or beneath a broiler until the outside skins are charred. Then let them cool slightly before peeling and removing the blackened skins. Remove the seeds and chop the chiles.

If your soup or stew is too spicy, do not panic. One remedy is to offer a dairy drink or condiment, such as milk or yogurt. Dairy products contain casein, an enzyme that washes away the capsaicin, the element that produces the chile's notorious heat. Another remedy may be to invite your chile-loving friends over and throw a party. To some people, hot food is a cause célèbre. Here is a guide to the chiles called for in *Vegetarian Soup Cuisine.*

Cayenne: This long red slender chile has a piquant, intense flavor. Fresh cayenne peppers are used in Creole gumbos and African and Asian soups. Cayennes are often dried and ground into powder.

Chipotle: These are large jalapeño peppers that have been dried and smoked. They are typically available canned in a tomato-like sauce and ready to use. Chipotles are also sold dried and air packed. (Soak the air-packed chiles for at least thirty minutes in warm water before using.) Smoky chipotle chiles make a good flavor substitute for bacon, pork, and ham.

Jalapeño: These dark green or red chiles have a thick flesh and are shaped like a miniature torpedo. They are the most versatile and widely available chiles on the market today. Jalapeños vary from mild to moderately hot.

New Mexico: These tapered green and red chiles have a fruity, addictive heat. Primarily grown in the American Southwest, New Mexico chiles are almost always roasted prior to adding to soups, chilies, *posoles,* and stews. When dried, they are tied into holiday *ristra* wreaths.

Poblano: This large, dark forest green pod has a broad anvil curvaceous shape. Poblanos are often roasted prior to adding to soups and chili. They have a raisinlike flavor and an endearing level of heat. Dried poblanos are called ancho chiles.

Red Fresno: These chiles are close cousins to red jalapeños, only slightly hotter. Red Fresno chiles have broad shoulders that taper to a point. They are available on a seasonal basis.

Scotch Bonnets and Habaneros: These are considered by many to be the world's hottest chiles, the crème de la crème of fiery peppers. They have curvy, contorted shapes, like miniature lanterns, and come in bright orange, yellow, green, and fire-engine red colors. First comes a ferocious burn, followed by a floral halo, then numbness, and finally (to some), bliss. These chiles are prevalent in Caribbean, Yucatan, and South American soups and stews. To tame the roar, the chiles are often punctured with a fork and simmered in a broth; at the end, they are removed and cut into strips and served on the side as a garnish.

Serrano: This pointy, narrow pepper has a dense core of seeds and sharp, biting heat. Serranos are popular in Mexican soups and stews.

Rice, Grains, and Pasta

This trio of starches adds body, flavor, and nutrients to a plethora of soups and stews, from minestrone to mushroom barley, gumbo to Mexican noodle. These starches also offer a lowfat way to thicken the soup pot without adding cream or butter. A few tablespoons are usually all that is needed; a little goes a long way. Grains, rice, and pasta contribute valuable complex carbohydrates and transform a bowl of soup into a full-fledged meal.

Arborio: This short-grained Italian rice is best known for its role in risotto, a creamy rice dish. The pearly white grain naturally thickens soups after twenty to thirty minutes in the broth.

Aromatic Rice: This family of rices includes basmati, jasmine, Texmati, Jasmati, wild pecan, and Uncle Ben's Aromatica. They have a nutty flavor and popcornlike aroma; the grains tend to be long and slender. Aromatic rices are natural accompaniments to curry soups, spicy bean soups, gumbos, and chilies. Make a small mound of cooked rice in the bowl and pour on the soup.

White Long Grain Rice and Parboiled Rice: The outer bran layer of the grain has been removed in the milling process, leaving a polished white grain. Some nutrients are lost in the milling, but the rice is later enriched. (Parboiled rice undergoes a slightly different process and retains more of the nutrients.) White rice takes fifteen to twenty minutes to cook and should be added to the soup near the finish.

Whole Grain Rices: These rices still have their nutrient-rich bran layer in tact. Varieties include brown rice, Wehani, black rice, and brown basmati rice. Whole grain rices hold up well over long cooking times—most take forty to fifty minutes to cook.

Pearl Barley: This mild-flavored grain adds bulk and body to the soup broth and blends well with mushroom soups, pea soups, and bean soups. Barley takes about fifty minutes to cook.

Quinoa: Pronounced *keen-wa,* this ancient grain is grown in the highlands of South America. Quinoa is tiny and ring-shaped with a faint nutty flavor; it greatly expands when cooked. Like white rice, it cooks in about fifteen minutes. Before cooking, rinse quinoa thoroughly to wash away the natural, bitter-tasting resin that coats the grains.

Wild Rice: This dark, slender grain is really the seed of a native American aquatic grass, not a rice. It has a firm, chewy texture, strong nutty flavor, and grassy aroma. Add it to long-cooking soups and stews; it cooks in about fifty minutes.

Asian Pastas: These include rice noodles (or rice sticks), buckwheat noodles (soba), quick-cooking somen, linguini-like udon noodles, and clear cellophane noodles (also called bean thread noodles). They all make fine additions to broths, especially to aromatic soups flavored with coconut, lime juice, or soy sauce.

Couscous: This is actually a tiny grainlike pasta made of fine semolina flour. Couscous cooks in about ten minutes so it should be added at the very end of the soup or stew. It is a staple of North African and Moroccan cuisine.

Pasta: Almost any pasta can be added to the soup pot. However, miniature pastas are less likely to commandeer the soup than larger pastas. Look for tubettini, ditalini, small soup shells, mini-spirals, small cheese tortellinis, and orzo (or rosa marina). To keep the pasta from bloating, add to the soup during the last ten to fifteen minutes of the cooking time.

Beans, Peas, and Lentils

Legumes are nutritional lodestars, packed with dietary fiber, protein, and complex carbohydrates, and are naturally low in fat and sodium. Legumes make you feel sated and give you energy. They are stellar staples in the new soup cuisine.

Beans: Just about every bean imaginable can be added to soups, stews, and chilies. Black beans, red kidney beans, small and large white beans, chickpeas, black-eyed peas —you name the bean, there's a potential soup in its future. Beans also have a global following: almost every country has a bean-inspired soup meal on their national menu, from Italian *pasta e fagioli* and Brazilian black bean soup to Jamaican red pea soup, Middle Eastern and Indian lentil stews, and countless others.

Dried beans should be sorted over and examined for sand and pebbles and then soaked first in plenty of water for at least four hours (preferably overnight) before cooking. Always drain the soaked beans and cook them in fresh water. Most beans take one to two hours to cook. Do not add salt, acidic ingredients, or tomato products to the beans while they cook—their shells will harden and they will ultimately take longer to become tender. Wait until the finish.

About 1 1/2 cups of cooked beans is the equivalent to one 15-ounce can of beans, drained. Canned beans need only to be reheated when blended into a soup or chili and should be added during the last ten to fifteen minutes of the cooking time. For more information, pick up a copy of *Lean Bean Cuisine,* the definitive guide to the humble legumes.

Lentils: There are several kinds of lentils, including brown, green, red, and yellow varieties. Lentils have a narrow, oval shape similar to a thin disk or lens. They are staples in Indian, Middle Eastern, North African, and European soups and stews. Lentils do not require presoaking, but if they are really old, soaking for a few hours will partially cut down on the cooking time. Lentils take about forty-five minutes to cook; red lentils take a little less time.

Split Peas: These are whole green or yellow peas that have been split along a natural break. Split peas cook to a pureed consistency and are a favorite ingredient in thick

European soups and stews. They take one to one-and-a-half hours to cook, and like lentils, should be soaked ahead of time if they are well aged.

Soup Greens

Leafy green vegetables are not just for tossed salads and garnishes anymore. There is a wide selection of nutritious and flavorful greens that add appealing textures and striking colors to the tureen. Many greens need only to be rinsed, coarsely chopped, and added to the pot ten or fifteen minutes before the soup is finished. Dark leafy greens are especially high in vitamin A and beta carotene, a cancer-fighting antioxidant.

Throughout *Vegetarian Soup Cuisine,* the term "chiffonade" comes up. This is a way of preparing greens for the soup: Roll up three or four leaves at a time and thinly slice the roll. This "ribbon cutting" is a fast and efficient way to slice leafy greens up for the soup pot.

Here is a summary of the leafy greens most often used in soups. Many of these leafy vegetables are interchangeable.

Beet Greens: The leafy green tops of beet roots add color and a slight mustard flavor to soups and stews. Look for beet greens with a healthy, unblemished appearance and untorn leaves.

Bok Choy: This is a Chinese leaf with floppy green leaves attached to a wide white stem. It has a mild cabbage flavor. Tat soi and pat soi are smaller, but similar, greens.

Chard: There is red chard and green chard; they are also called Swiss chard. Chard has a crunchy texture with a mild mustard flavor. Red chard has beet-red veins running throughout the leaf. (Chard is actually a kind of beet that was bred for its leafy tops.)

Collard Greens: These large, faded green, sturdy leaves are best cut into ribbons (chiffonade style) and added to long-cooking soups and stews; they take twenty to thirty minutes to cook. Collards are a favorite green in Southern soups and are extremely nutritious.

Escarole: This wide, pale green leaf has a mildly bitter flavor. It is used in Italian soups and can replace kale or chard in most recipes.

Kale: Although often used as a garnish, this crinkly, olive green leaf makes an excellent soup staple. Its cousin red Russian kale has a flatter, purplish green leaf and is also a good soup green.

Mustard Greens and **Turnip Greens:** These greens have strong mustardy and slightly bitter undertones. They are a favorite green vegetable in Southern soups and stews.

Winter Squash and Root Vegetables

There is a bounty of winter squash and root vegetables that inspire mellifluous soups and stews. Winter squash are rich in beta carotene and essential nutrients, while root vegetables offer valuable complex carbohydrates and substance. In addition, well-cooked winter squash and root vegetables meld smoothly into the soup pot and create a creamy broth. Once mashed or pureed into the soup, there is little need for fat-laden cream.

Beet Roots: These magenta bulbs lend their raspberry hue to tomato soups, root vegetable bisques, and myriad borschts. Choose beets with their green tops still attached—the beet greens can also be added to the soup. Stay away from the canned versions.

Buttercup Squash: These dark green gourds are shaped like a dense turban. They have a sweet-potato-like, buttery flesh. Buttercup squash are interchangeable with most other winter squash.

Butternut Squash: Easily one of the most common and versatile squash, butternuts are long, narrow, and tan-skinned with bell-shaped ends. They are widely available and meld well into numerous soups and stews. Simply peel the thin skin and dice like a potato.

Leeks: These large, fibrous stalky root vegetables add a subtle onion flavor to soups and stews, notably vichyssoise. Soak and rinse the leeks thoroughly before cooking to remove grit and sand trapped between the green leaves.

Parsnips: This off-white root resembles a well-aged carrot. Parsnips have a mildly sweet flavor and firm texture. They are best combined with potatoes.

Potatoes: There are so many kinds—white, red, sweet potatoes (these are not really in the potato family, they're actually roots), Yukon Gold, and even blue potatoes. About the only potatoes to avoid in soups are baking potatoes, which tend to mash up fast. For most soups and chowders, it's a good idea to skip the peeling and leave the skin on—there are valuable nutrients in the skin.

Pumpkin: The small, dense sugar pie varieties are best for soups and chowders. Cut the pumpkins in half, peel the thin skin, remove the seeds, and dice the flesh. Large field pumpkins (jack-o'-lanterns) can be used but are more seedy.

Red Kuri Squash: Also called Golden Hubbard, this burnt orange–red squash has a thin skin and rich, sweet, dense flesh. When in season, they are a treasured staple in the new soup cuisine.

Rutabagas: These large, softball-shaped, light brownish bulbs have a firm creamy flesh and mild cauliflower-radish flavor. Peel the thin coating of wax (paraffin) before dicing and cooking.

Turnips: These portly roots shaped like spinning tops have a light purple band around the top and off-white flesh. Turnips have a radish and mustard flavor and firm texture. The greens also make a valuable addition to soups.

West Indian Pumpkin: Also called calabaza, this large, Hubbard-like squash has bright orange, dense flesh and sweet-potato-like flavor. The pumpkin is a popular year-round staple in Caribbean and Hispanic cooking. Look for it in Caribbean markets and well-stocked supermarkets—it is often cut up and sold in wedges.

Flavored Liquids

There are several lowfat ways to intensify and enhance a soup or stew at the last minute.

Balsamic Vinegar: A few tablespoons of this well-aged vinegar brings a smooth, slightly acidic surge of flavor to beet soups, leafy green soups, and thick tomato soups.

Lemon Juice: A squeeze of fresh lemon does wonders for mild, flat soups in need of a quick pick-me-up. Lemon is especially welcome in vichyssoise, dairy-based soups, and grain stews and soups. Lime juice is welcome in chilled fruit soups and coconut soups.

Miso: This nutrient-rich paste of fermented soybeans, salt, and grains is used extensively in Japanese soups. It has a mild presence and is said to aid in digestion. The most common varieties—barley (red), rice (white), and soy (dark)—are sold in natural food stores and Asian markets. Do not boil the soup once the miso has been added.

Red Wine Vinegar: The slightest amount of vinegar will perk up a bland soup or stew, and all without a trace of fat. Almost any brand of wine vinegar can be used, as well as rice vinegar, cider vinegar, champagne vinegar, and sherry vinegar.

Soy Sauce: This dark, salty, fermented liquid brings flavor to Asian soups, especially broths with coconut, lime, or ginger. Choose a low-sodium soy sauce or tamari without added sugar or monosodium glutamate.

Bottled Hot Sauces: Piquant liquids derived from chile peppers are indispensable in the kitchen. Tabasco sauce is a standard condiment on many tables, more so than salt and pepper. Other sauces include Scotch bonnet, habanero, jalapeño, and cayenne peppers. Hot sauces are healthful replacements for salty and buttery flavors, and a few drops go a long way.

Chapter 3

A Harvest of Autumn Soups and Stews

Autumn means many things to many people. It is a time for harvest festivals and football games, picking apples and raking leaves. The days are shorter and cooler, yet distant horizons are festooned with a fireworks of foliage. The lazy days of summer give way to the reflective afternoons of autumn.

Autumn is a glorious time for soup connoisseurs. The hills and fields are alive with soup-friendly vegetables. There are all kinds of large, motley squash—butternut, pumpkin, blue Hubbard, red kuri, buttercup, and others—all of which inspire delectable soups and stews. Verdant leafy greens such as kale, spinach, red Russian kale, and chard are in abundant supply. Root vegetables also begin to show up with more frequency.

In this chapter these humble, unpretentious staples are transformed into an array of appetizing creations: Curried Squash and Autumn Greens Soup, Beet Vichyssoise, and Spicy Pumpkin and Moroccan Couscous Stew are some of the tantalizing tureens. The soup kitchen overfloweth with adventurous ethnic fare such as Haitian Hot Pot, Spicy Eggplant Ratatouille, and Succotash Squash Soup.

Autumn is a great time to enjoy both rustic and eclectic soups and stews. These seasonal soups will satisfy the appetite, take the sting out of summer's demise, and fortify the spirit for the chilly winter looming around the corner.

Sweet Potato and Leek Bisque

Here is proof that a bisque does not have to be loaded with heavy cream or butter to bring delicious pleasure to the palate. The natural essence of sweet potatoes, leeks, and herbs carries the day.

1	tablespoon canola oil
1	medium yellow onion, diced
2	cups rinsed and chopped leeks
2	medium carrots, peeled and diced
2	cloves garlic, minced
4	cups water
4	cups peeled, coarsely chopped sweet potatoes
1/4	cup dry white wine
1 1/2	tablespoons dried parsley
1/2	teaspoon salt
1/2	teaspoon ground white pepper
1	cup lowfat or whole milk
1/4	cup chopped fresh chives or scallions (for garnish)

In a large saucepan heat the oil. Add the onion, leeks, carrots, and garlic, and sauté for about 5 minutes. Add the water, sweet potatoes, wine, and dried seasonings, and bring to a simmer. Cook over low heat for 25 to 30 minutes, stirring occasionally. Remove the soup from the heat and let cool for about 5 minutes.

Transfer the soup to a blender or food processor fitted with a steel blade and puree until smooth. Return the soup to the pan and stir in the milk. Bring the soup to a gentle simmer and then remove from the heat.

Ladle into bowls and serve hot or chill for later. Sprinkle the chives over the soup before serving.

Yield: 6 servings

Caldo Verde (Portuguese Kale and Potato Soup)

Caldo verde means "green soup" in Portuguese. As part of a fund-raising dinner for a local charity, I served this simple, but pleasing, soup to almost three hundred people. Spicing such a large quantity of soup was a real challenge, but it worked; the crowd cleaned their bowls.

1	tablespoon olive oil
1	medium yellow onion, chopped
2	or 3 cloves garlic, minced
4	cups water
4	cups diced white potatoes (peeled if desired)
1/2	teaspoon salt
1/2	teaspoon ground white or black pepper
2	cups chopped, packed kale or chard
1	(15-ounce) can white kidney beans (cannellini), drained
1/4	cup diced roasted sweet red peppers or pimentos
1/4	cup chopped fresh parsley

In a large saucepan heat the oil. Add the onion and garlic, and sauté for about 4 minutes. Add the water, potatoes, and dried seasonings, and cook for 20 to 25 minutes over medium heat, stirring occasionally.

Stir in the kale, beans, roasted peppers, and parsley, and cook for 10 minutes more. Turn off the heat and let stand for about 10 minutes. To thicken, mash the potatoes against the side of the pan.

Ladle the soup into bowls and serve with warm crusty bread.

Yield: 6 servings

Curried Squash and Autumn Greens Soup

The glorious greens of autumn—kale, chard, red Russian kale, and many others—make great additions to soups and stews. Here they team up with two other notable fall crops, squash and pumpkin. Warm curry spices give this harvest soup an upbeat personality.

1	tablespoon canola oil
1	large yellow onion, diced
1	cup sliced celery
2	tomatoes or 4 plum tomatoes, diced
3	to 4 cloves garlic, minced
2	teaspoons minced fresh ginger
1	tablespoon curry powder
2	teaspoons ground cumin
1	teaspoon ground coriander
1	teaspoon salt
1/2	teaspoon ground black pepper
4	cups peeled and diced red kuri, sugar pie pumpkin, or butternut squash
5	cups water
2	to 3 cups coarsely chopped spinach, red Russian kale, or kale

In a large saucepan heat the oil. Add the onion and celery, and sauté for about 5 minutes. Add the tomatoes, garlic, and ginger, and sauté for 3 to 4 minutes more. Stir in the seasonings and cook for 1 minute more over low heat, stirring frequently. Add the squash and water, and cook for about 25 minutes over medium-low heat until the squash is tender. Stir in the greens and cook for 10 minutes more over low heat. Let the soup cool slightly.

Transfer the mixture to a blender or food processor fitted with a steel blade and process for about 10 seconds, until smooth. Pour into serving bowls and serve hot. Cucumber Yogurt Raita (page 241) makes a natural accompaniment.

Yield: 6 servings

Parsnip and Exotic Greens Tureen

In the late spring and early fall, the farmers' market yields a bounty of exotic soup greens—mizuna, red Russian kale, and frisee are some of the leafy enticements. More than once I have stumbled home from the market and crammed my refrigerator with unwieldy bunches of greens. In this verdant soup meal, soup greens join up with hardy parsnips and potatoes.

1	tablespoon canola oil
1	medium yellow onion, diced
1	cup sliced celery
2	cloves garlic, minced
6	cups water
2	cups peeled and diced parsnips
2	cups peeled and diced white potatoes
1	teaspoon dried thyme
3/4	teaspoon salt
1/2	teaspoon ground black pepper
4	cups chopped mixed leafy greens, such as mizuna, frisee, red Russian kale, or pat choi
1/4	cup chopped fresh parsley

In a large saucepan, heat the oil. Add the onion, celery, and garlic, and sauté for 4 minutes. Add the water, parsnips, potatoes, and dried seasonings, and bring to a simmer. Cook for 20 to 25 minutes over medium-low heat, stirring occasionally, until the vegetables are tender. Stir in the greens and parsley and cook for 5 to 10 minutes more.

To thicken, transfer half of the soup to a blender or food processor fitted with a steel blade and puree until smooth. Return the pureed soup to the pan and keep hot until ready to serve.

Yield: 4 to 6 servings

Haitian Hot Pot

Haitian cuisine is a melting pot of African, Creole, French, and native island food. Haitian soups often include hardy squash, potatoes, turnips, and red beans. Hot chile peppers infuse the broth with a fiery flair and give new meaning to the term "tropical heat wave."

1	tablespoon canola oil
1	medium yellow onion, diced
1	large green or red bell pepper, seeded and diced
1	stalk celery, sliced
2	cloves garlic, minced
1/2	Scotch bonnet or 2 jalapeño peppers, seeded and minced
8	cups hot water
2	cups peeled and diced butternut squash or West Indian pumpkin
2	cups coarsely chopped white potatoes
1	medium turnip, peeled and diced
1	tablespoon dried parsley
1	teaspoon dried thyme
1	teaspoon salt
1/4	teaspoon turmeric
1	(15-ounce) can red kidney beans, drained

In a large saucepan heat the oil. Add the onion, bell pepper, celery, garlic, and chile(s), and sauté for 5 to 7 minutes. Add the water, squash, potatoes, turnips, and seasonings, and cook for about 45 minutes over low heat, stirring occasionally. Stir in the beans and cook for about 5 minutes more. To thicken, mash the squash and potatoes against the side of the pan with the back of a spoon.

Let the soup stand for about 10 minutes before serving. Ladle into bowls and serve with warm bread to mop up the flavors.

Yield: 8 to 10 servings

Soup Tips

Scotch bonnet peppers are considered by many to be the world's hottest chiles and should be used with caution. They are available in the produce section of well-stocked supermarkets and Caribbean markets. Dasheen, a starchy tropical tuber, may be used in place of potatoes.

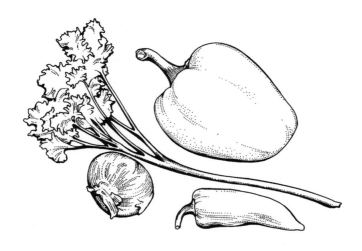

Curried Pumpkin Bisque

While the Caribbean is known for mangoes, bananas, and other tropical fruits, it is also home to the West Indian pumpkin, a huge Hubbard-like squash with bright orange flesh. In fact, a plethora of pumpkin soups simmer year-round in Caribbean kitchens. I first tasted this curry-scented soup while visiting St. Lucia.

1	tablespoon canola oil
1	medium yellow onion, diced
1	cup sliced celery
4	cloves garlic, minced
2	teaspoons minced fresh ginger
1	jalapeño or other hot chile, seeded and minced
2	large tomatoes, diced
2	to 3 teaspoons curry powder
1 1/2	teaspoons ground cumin
1	teaspoon salt
1/2	teaspoon ground black pepper
1/4	teaspoon ground cloves
4	cups peeled and diced West Indian pumpkin or other winter squash
5	cups water

In a large saucepan heat the oil. Add the onion, celery, garlic, ginger, and jalapeño and sauté for about 5 minutes. Add the tomatoes and sauté for 2 to 3 minutes more. Stir in the seasonings and cook for 1 minute more over low heat, stirring frequently. Add the pumpkin and water and bring to a simmer. Cook for 30 to 35 minutes over medium-low heat, stirring occasionally, until the pumpkin melds into the soup.

Let the soup cool slightly. Transfer to a blender or food processor fitted with a steel blade and process for 10 seconds, until smooth. Ladle into bowls and serve with Skillet Roti Bread (page 249) or Indian flat bread.

Yield: 6 servings

Soup Tips
West Indian pumpkin, also called calabaza, is available in well-stocked supermarkets and Latin American grocery stores. Sugar pie pumpkin or butternut, Hubbard, or red kuri squash may be substituted.

Succotash Squash Soup

"This soup tastes Southern," remarked one friend with a Southern drawl. Succotash—the combination of beans and corn—and squash go way, way back. Native Americans grew the crops together: bean vines climbed up tall stalks of corn while squash crawled along the ground in between plants. The "three sisters" naturally go together in soups and stews.

1   tablespoon canola oil
1   medium yellow onion, diced
1   green or red bell pepper, seeded and diced
2   stalks celery, chopped
2   to 3 cloves garlic, minced
4   cups water or vegetable stock
3   cups peeled and diced butternut squash or buttercup squash
2   tablespoons dried parsley
2   teaspoons ground cumin
3/4 teaspoon salt
1/2 teaspoon ground black pepper
2   cups green lima beans (about 10 ounces frozen)
2   cups corn kernels, fresh or frozen
3   or 4 scallions, chopped (for garnish)

In a large saucepan heat the oil. Add the onion, bell pepper, celery, and garlic, and sauté for 5 to 7 minutes. Add the water, squash, and seasonings, and cook over medium-low heat for about 20 minutes, stirring occasionally, until the squash is tender. Add the lima beans and corn and return to a simmer; cook for 10 to 15 minutes more, stirring occasionally.

Remove from the heat and let stand for several minutes. To thicken, mash the squash against the side of the pan with the back of a spoon.

Ladle the soup into bowls and sprinkle the scallions over the top.

Yield: 8 servings

Sante Fe Chile, Corn, and Squash Chowder

After visiting Sante Fe, my appreciation for Southwestern cuisine was stoked to a full-fledged passion. I gained a better understanding of native squash, beans, corn, cilantro, and other humble staples. Most of all, I discovered the thrills of cooking with New Mexico chiles, the slender pods with a fruity resonance and entrancing, mesmerizing heat.

1	tablespoon canola oil
1	medium yellow onion, diced
1	red bell pepper, seeded and diced
1	large stalk celery, chopped
2	to 3 cloves garlic, minced
1	or 2 roasted New Mexico red chiles, peeled, seeded, and chopped
6	cups water or vegetable stock
4	cups peeled and diced butternut squash
1¹/₂	tablespoons dried parsley
2	teaspoons dried oregano
1¹/₂	teaspoons ground cumin
1	teaspoon salt
¹/₂	teaspoon ground black pepper
2	cups corn kernels, fresh or frozen
2	tablespoons chopped fresh cilantro
3	or 4 scallions, chopped (for garnish)

In a large saucepan heat the oil. Add the onion, bell pepper, celery, garlic, and New Mexico chile(s), and sauté for about 5 minutes. Add the water, squash, and seasonings (except the cilantro), and cook over medium-low heat for about 20 minutes, stirring occasionally, until the squash is tender.

Stir in the corn and return to a simmer; cook for 10 to 15 minutes more, stirring occasionally. Stir in the cilantro.

Remove from the heat and let stand for several minutes before serving. To thicken, mash the squash against the side of the pan with the back of a spoon.

Ladle the soup into bowls and sprinkle the scallions over the top.

Yield: 8 servings

Soup Tips

New Mexico chiles are available on a limited seasonal basis. While there is no real substitute, a jalapeño or poblano chile may also be used in the soup. For tips on roasting chiles, see page (17).

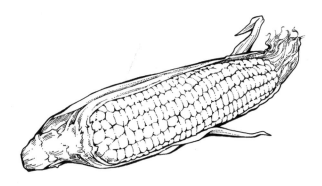

Asian Greens and Roasted Tofu Soup

There is a diverse family of healthful Asian leafy greens—bok choy, napa, Chinese cabbage, pat soi, and red sen choy to name a few. Here the greens are combined with roasted tofu in a lightly flavored broth. (Roasting the tofu gives it a firm, chewy texture.)

1/2	pound extra firm tofu, cut into 1/2-inch cubes
1	tablespoon canola oil
1	medium yellow onion, chopped
2	medium carrots, peeled and slivered at an angle
2	cloves garlic, minced
2	teaspoons minced fresh ginger
6	cups water or vegetable stock
2	or 3 tablespoons low-sodium soy sauce
2	teaspoons rice vinegar
1	teaspoon hot sesame oil
1/4	teaspoon ground black pepper
2	cups coarsely chopped bok choy, pat soi, or red sen choy
2	cups coarsely chopped Chinese cabbage or napa cabbage
1	cup snow pea pods, trimmed and halved

Preheat the oven to 375°F.

Place the tofu on a lightly greased baking pan and roast for 15 to 20 minutes in the oven until lightly browned. Turn the cubes after 10 minutes. Remove from the oven and let cool slightly.

In a large saucepan heat the oil. Add the onion, carrots, garlic, and ginger, and sauté for 5 minutes. Add the water, soy sauce, vinegar, sesame oil, black pepper, and tofu, and bring to a simmer. Cook over medium-low heat for about 15 minutes, stirring occasionally. Stir in the bok choy, cabbage greens, and snow peas, and cook for 10 to 15 minutes more, stirring occasionally. Let the soup stand for 10 minutes before serving.

Ladle into bowls and serve hot.

Yield: 6 servings

Soup Tips

To give the soup an earthy flavor, add 4 to 6 fresh shiitake or oyster mushrooms to the pan when sautéing the vegetables. Many of these greens are available at Asian grocery stores and well-stocked supermarkets.

Squash Callaloo Soup

The Caribbean comprises many islands, peoples, and cultures, but one soup is universal—callaloo. What is callaloo? It is a broad leafy green, treasured for its role in soups and stews. Every island has its own rendition and there is plenty of improvisation. This meatless version is fortified with butternut squash. While callaloo is difficult to find in the States, spinach or chard are close substitutes.

1	tablespoon canola oil
1	medium yellow onion, diced
2	or 3 cloves garlic, minced
1	or 2 jalapeño or other hot chiles, seeded and minced
5	cups water or vegetable stock
2	cups peeled and diced butternut squash or West Indian pumpkin
2	tablespoons dark rum
1	teaspoon dried thyme
1/2	teaspoon ground black pepper
1/2	teaspoon salt
1/4	teaspoon ground allspice
4	cups coarsely chopped fresh callaloo, spinach, or Swiss chard
1	cup lowfat coconut milk
2	tablespoons chopped fresh parsley

In a large saucepan heat the oil. Add the onion, garlic, and jalapeño, and sauté for 5 minutes. Stir in the water, squash, rum, and dried seasonings, and bring to a simmer. Cook over medium-low heat for 20 minutes, stirring occasionally. Stir in the greens, coconut milk, and parsley, and cook for 5 to 10 minutes more over low heat. To thicken, mash the squash against the side of the pan. Let stand for 10 minutes before serving.

Ladle into bowls and serve with Skillet Roti Bread (page 249).

Yield: 6 servings

Soup Tips
Callaloo can sometimes be found in Caribbean markets. West Indian pumpkin, also called calabaza, has a rich, dense orange flesh and is available in West Indian, Caribbean, or Hispanic markets and well-stocked supermarkets.

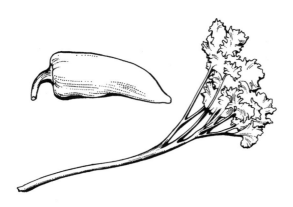

Spicy Eggplant Ratatouille

This piquant rendition of the classic Mediterranean stew is hearty, well-rounded, and wonderfully amplified with lively jalapeño peppers.

2	tablespoons canola oil
1	medium yellow onion, diced
1	medium eggplant, diced
1	green or red bell pepper, seeded and diced
2	cloves garlic, minced
2	jalapeños or other hot chiles, seeded and minced
4	cups water or vegetable stock
1	(14-ounce) can stewed tomatoes
1/4	cup tomato paste
1/4	cup dry red wine
1	tablespoon dried parsley (or 2 tablespoons chopped fresh parsley)
2	teaspoons dried oregano
1	teaspoon ground cumin
1/2	teaspoon ground black pepper
1/2	teaspoon salt

In a large saucepan heat the oil. Add the onion, eggplant, bell pepper, garlic, and chiles, and cook for about 10 minutes over medium heat, stirring frequently. Stir in the water, stewed tomatoes, tomato paste, wine, and seasonings, and bring to a simmer. Cook over medium-low heat for about 30 minutes, stirring occasionally. Let stand for 10 minutes before serving.

Ladle into bowls and serve with Corn Bread Croutons (page **242**) or whole grain bread.

Yield: 6 servings

Soup Tips

For added substance, add a 15-ounce can of white or red kidney beans (drained) to the soup 5 minutes before serving. If you prefer a mild soup, omit the chiles and add about 1/4 teaspoon black pepper.

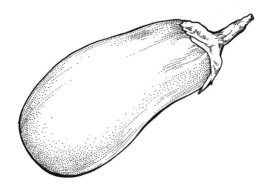

Mushroom, Barley, and Leafy Greens Soup

Barley and mushrooms share a natural affinity for each other. Everyone seems to have a memory of a favorite mushroom and barley soup. This meatless version is heightened with the introduction of verdant leafy greens and a touch of mustard.

1	tablespoon canola oil
12	ounces button mushrooms, sliced
1	medium yellow onion, diced
2	cloves garlic, minced
6	cups water
2	large carrots, peeled and diced
1/2	cup barley
1/4	cup dry white wine
2	teaspoons Dijon-style mustard
1 1/2	tablespoons dried parsley (or 3 tablespoons chopped fresh parsley)
1	teaspoon dried thyme
1	teaspoon salt
1/2	teaspoon ground black pepper
4	cups coarsely chopped and mixed kale and green chard
1	large lemon, cut into wedges (optional)

In a large saucepan heat the oil. Add the mushrooms, onion, and garlic, and cook for 8 to 10 minutes over medium heat, stirring frequently. Add the water, carrots, barley, wine, mustard, and seasonings. Cook for 50 minutes to 1 hour over low heat, stirring occasionally. Stir in the greens and cook for 5 to 10 minutes more. Let the soup stand for several minutes before serving.

Ladle into bowls and serve with dark bread. If you'd like, squeeze a wedge of lemon over the soup before serving.

Yield: 6 servings

Soup Tips
If red Russian kale or field spinach is available, it can also be used.

Autumn Harvest Stew

*When I close down the garden in late autumn and lament
the passing of yet another summer, the once fertile and lush
terrain becomes but a fond memory. All is not lost, however,
as I soon find consolation in the kitchen. The garden harvest
continues to bring pleasure through stews like this one.*

1	tablespoon canola oil
1	medium yellow onion, diced
2	stalks celery, chopped
2	or 3 cloves garlic, minced
2	large tomatoes, diced
1	tablespoon paprika
1	tablespoon dried oregano
1	teaspoon ground cumin
1/2	teaspoon salt
1/2	teaspoon ground black pepper
2	cups peeled, diced buttercup, butternut, or other winter squash
2	cups shredded red or green cabbage
5	cups water or vegetable stock
2	cups coarsely chopped red Russian kale or Swiss chard

In a large saucepan heat the oil. Add the onion, celery, and garlic, and sauté for 4 minutes. Add the tomatoes and seasonings, and cook for 3 to 4 minutes more over medium-low heat, stirring frequently, until the mixture resembles a thick pulp. Add the squash, cabbage, and water or vegetable stock and bring to a simmer. Cook for about 25 minutes, stirring occasionally, until the squash is tender. Stir in kale (or Swiss chard), and cook for 10 minutes more.

Ladle the stew into large serving bowls. Serve with jasmine rice, basmati rice, or another grain on the side. Lowfat sour cream makes a soothing topping.

Yield: 4 to 6 servings

Soup Tips

For a flavor nuance, simmer 3 or 4 whole branches of thyme and 2 or 3 whole red chile peppers in the soup. (Remove the thyme and chiles just before serving.)

Tarragon Carrot Bisque

Even in the most minuscule portions the herb tarragon will assert its distinctive anise-and-lavender-like presence. Here it artfully enhances this beta carotene-rich golden orange carrot soup.

1	tablespoon canola oil
1	medium yellow onion, diced
1	large stalk celery, chopped
2	cloves garlic, minced
5	cups water
3	cups peeled and diced carrots
1	medium white potato, peeled and diced
1/4	cup dry white wine
1	tablespoon dried parsley
1 1/2	teaspoons dried tarragon
3/4	teaspoon salt
1/2	teaspoon ground black pepper
1/4	teaspoon turmeric (optional)
1	cup lowfat milk, whole milk, or soy milk
1/4	cup chopped fresh chives (for garnish)

In a large saucepan heat the oil. Add the onion, celery, and garlic, and sauté for 5 to 7 minutes. Add the water, carrots, potato, wine, and dried seasonings, and bring to a simmer. Cook over medium-low heat for about 35 minutes, stirring occasionally. Stir in the milk and return to a simmer. Remove the soup from the heat and let cool for a few minutes. Transfer the soup to a blender or food processor fitted with a steel blade and puree until smooth.

Ladle into bowls and serve hot, or chill for later. To garnish, sprinkle chives over the soup before serving.

Yield: 6 to 8 servings

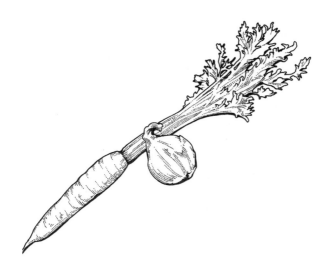

Two Grain and Winter Squash Soup

Grains make a great addition to a variety of soups. They are an excellent source of complex carbohydrates and give us long-lasting, well-balanced energy. They also offer a lowfat, low-sodium way to thicken soups. In this nourishing soup, chewy brown rice and barley complement the smooth, buttery consistency of winter squash.

1	tablespoon canola oil
1	medium yellow onion, diced
1	celery stalk, chopped
12	button mushrooms, sliced
2	cloves garlic, minced
7	to 8 cups water
2	cups peeled and diced butternut squash, red kuri, or other winter squash
1/4	cup brown rice
1/4	cup barley
1/4	cup dry white wine
1 1/2	tablespoons dried parsley (or 4 tablespoons chopped fresh parsley)
2	teaspoons dried oregano
1	teaspoon salt
1/2	teaspoon ground black pepper

In a large saucepan heat the oil. Add the onion, celery, mushrooms, and garlic, and cook for 8 to 10 minutes over medium heat, stirring frequently. Stir in the water, squash, rice, barley, wine, and seasonings, and bring to a simmer. Cook for 50 minutes to 1 hour over low heat, stirring occasionally.

Let the soup stand for several minutes before serving. Ladle into bowls and serve with dark bread.

Yield: 6 servings

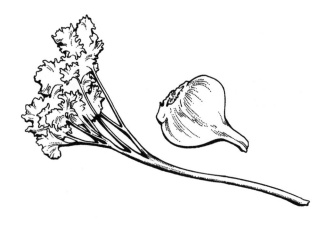

Root Greens and Brown Rice Soup

Root greens are ideal candidates for the soup pot. The leafy tops attached to root vegetables—beet greens, turnip greens, even carrot tops—supply mustardlike flavors, inviting colors, and as a bonus, are nutrient rich and inexpensive. This soup, thickened with brown rice, is delicious and soothing.

1	tablespoon canola oil
1	medium yellow onion, diced
1	large stalk celery, chopped
2	cloves garlic, minced
6	cups water
2	medium carrots, peeled and diced
1	medium turnip or parsnip, peeled and diced
1/4	cup brown rice
1	tablespoon dried parsley
1	teaspoon salt
1/2	teaspoon ground black pepper
2	cups coarsely chopped turnip greens
2	cups coarsely chopped beet greens or red chard (cut chiffonade style)
1/2	cup chopped carrot tops or celery leaves

In a large saucepan heat the oil. Add the onion, celery, and garlic, and sauté for 5 to 7 minutes. Add the water, carrots, turnip or parsnip, rice, and dried seasonings, and bring to a simmer. Cook over medium-low heat for 25 to 30 minutes, stirring occasionally. Stir in the turnip greens, beet greens, and carrot tops, and cook for 15 minutes more over low heat. Remove the soup from the heat and let cool for a few minutes.

Ladle into bowls and serve with warm bread.

Yield: 4 to 6 servings

West Indian Pumpkin Sancocho

Sancocho is a stew found in the Caribbean and Central America. This meatless version is fortified with West Indian pumpkin, a magnificent squash with bright orange flesh, and dasheen (also called taro), a starchy, potatolike tropical tuber.

1	tablespoon canola oil
1	medium yellow onion, diced
1	green bell pepper, seeded and diced
2	cloves garlic, minced
1	jalapeño or other hot chile, seeded and minced (optional)
1	large tomato, diced
1 1/2	tablespoons dried parsley
2	teaspoons curry powder
1 1/2	teaspoons cumin
1	teaspoon dried thyme
1/2	teaspoon ground black pepper
1/2	teaspoon salt
4	cups water
2	medium carrots, peeled and diced
2	cups peeled and diced dasheen or white potatoes
2	cups peeled and diced West Indian pumpkin or butternut squash

In a large saucepan heat the oil. Add the onion, bell pepper, garlic, and jalapeño, and sauté for 5 minutes. Stir in the tomato and seasonings, and cook for 2 minutes more over low heat. Add the water, carrots, dasheen, and pumpkin, and bring to a simmer. Cook over medium-low heat for 40 to 45 minutes, stirring occasionally, until the vegetables are tender. Remove from the heat and let stand for 10 minutes before serving. To thicken, mash the pumpkin and dasheen against the side of the pan with the back of a spoon.

Ladle into bowls and serve with Skillet Roti Bread (page 249).

Yield: 4 servings

Soup Tips

Look for dasheen and West Indian pumpkin (also called calabaza) in Caribbean and Hispanic markets or in specialty produce sections of well-stocked grocery stores. Hubbard or butternut squash may be substituted for West Indian pumpkin.

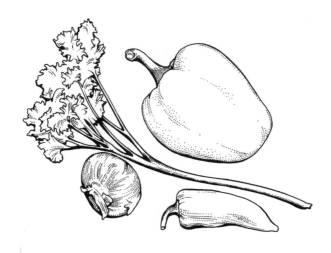

Porotos Granados

This robust stew from Chile includes three ancient American crops: pumpkin, corn, and beans. (Porotos granados loosely means "choice beans.") These three indigenous staples can be traced back to the Inca civilization and are still grown and eaten together throughout the Americas.

1	tablespoon canola oil
1	medium yellow onion, diced
2	or 3 cloves garlic, minced
1	jalapeño pepper, seeded and minced (optional)
2	large tomatoes, diced
1	tablespoon paprika
1 1/2	tablespoons dried parsley
2	teaspoons dried oregano
1	teaspoon ground cumin
1/2	teaspoon ground black pepper
1/2	teaspoon salt
4	cups peeled and diced pumpkin, red kuri or butternut squash
4	cups water
1 1/2	cups corn kernels, fresh or frozen
1	(15-ounce) can cranberry beans or red kidney beans, drained

In a large saucepan heat the oil. Add the onion, garlic, and jalapeño, and sauté for about 4 minutes. Add the tomatoes and seasonings, and cook for 3 to 4 minutes more, stirring frequently. Add the pumpkin and water, and cook for about 30 minutes, stirring occasionally, until the pumpkin is tender. Stir in the corn and beans, and cook for about 10 minutes more over low heat. To thicken, mash the pumpkin against the side of the pan.

Serve with a side of quinoa or brown rice.

Yield: 4 to 6 servings

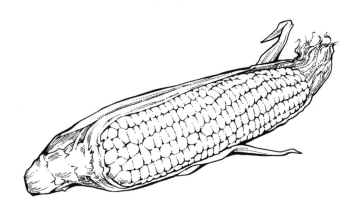

Autumn Squash and Eggplant Chowder

In a perfect world, those big, hefty squash harvested in late autumn would be available all year long. Blue Hubbard, red kuri, calabaza, butternut, and others are loaded with beta carotene and make perfect fodder for soups, stews, and chowders. Here they combine with eggplant for an uncommonly delicious chowder.

1	tablespoon canola oil
1	medium yellow onion, diced
1	red or green bell pepper, seeded and diced
2	cups diced eggplant
2	celery stalks, chopped
2	cloves garlic, minced
1	jalapeño or other hot chile, seeded and minced (optional)
4	cups water
2	cups peeled and diced butternut, red kuri, or Hubbard squash
2	teaspoons dried oregano
1	teaspoon paprika
1	teaspoon dried thyme
1	teaspoon ground cumin
1/2	teaspoon salt
1	cup whole or lowfat milk

In a large saucepan heat the oil. Add the onion, bell pepper, eggplant, celery, garlic, and jalapeño, and cook over medium heat for about 10 minutes. Add the water, squash, and seasonings, and cook for about 20 minutes over medium-low heat, stirring occasionally.

Stir in the milk and return to a gentle simmer. To thicken, mash the squash against the side of the pan with the back of a spoon. Remove from the heat and let stand for 5 to 10 minutes before serving.

Jasmine or basmati rice makes a desirable dinner accompaniment.

Yield: 6 servings

Spicy Pumpkin and Moroccan Couscous Stew

Pumpkin melds well with couscous, a tiny grainlike pasta prevalent in Moroccan and North African cuisine. This stew is heightened with harissa, an aromatic spice paste with a gratifying level of heat.

1	tablespoon canola oil or olive oil
1	medium yellow onion, diced
1	red bell pepper, seeded and diced
2	or 3 cloves garlic, minced
2	large ripe tomatoes, diced
1 1/2	to 2 tablespoons *harissa* (Moroccan chili paste)
4	cups water
2	cups peeled and diced sugar pie pumpkin or other winter squash
1/2	teaspoon salt
1	(15-ounce) can chickpeas, drained
1/2	cup couscous
2	to 3 tablespoons chopped fresh parsley

In a large saucepan heat the oil. Add the onion, bell pepper, and garlic, and sauté for 4 minutes. Add the tomato and sauté for 2 minutes more. Add the *harissa* and sauté for 1 minute more. Stir in the water, squash, and salt, and bring to a simmer. Cook for 25 minutes over medium-low heat, stirring occasionally, until the squash is tender.

Stir in the chickpeas, couscous, and parsley, and cover. Let the stew sit for 10 minutes before serving.

Stir the stew and ladle into bowls.

Yield: 4 to 6 servings

Soup Tips

If pumpkin is not available, try butternut squash. *Harissa* is available in the specialty section of well-stocked supermarkets. If unavailable, try adding 1 teaspoon each of ground cumin and coriander and ¼ teaspoon cayenne pepper.

Thai Coconut Mushroom and Cellophane Noodle Soup

Thai soups are delicate, complexly flavored, and often spicy. Nutty coconut coats the tongue, lime and lemon grass offer a ray of tanginess, and panang curry paste asserts a tingly (but fleeting) heat. I've added meaty portobello mushroom caps in place of the traditional chicken or seafood. Cellophane noodles (also called bean thread noodles) make this soup an ample meal.

2	teaspoons canola or peanut oil
1	small yellow onion, finely chopped
1	small red bell pepper, seeded and chopped
6	ounces portobello mushroom caps or button mushrooms, sliced
1	clove garlic, minced
2	teaspoons minced fresh lemon grass
1	to 1 1/2 teaspoons Thai panang or green curry paste
1	(14-ounce) can lowfat coconut milk
1	cup water
2	tablespoons light soy sauce
	Juice of 1/2 lime
1	teaspoon cornstarch
1	teaspoon warm water
1/2	ounce cellophane (or bean thread) noodles
2	tablespoons chopped cilantro
2	scallions, chopped (for garnish)

In a large saucepan heat the oil. Add the onion, bell pepper, mushrooms, garlic, and lemon grass, and sauté for 5 to 7 minutes. Stir in the curry paste and cook for 1 minute more over low heat, stirring frequently. Stir in the coconut milk, water, soy sauce, and lime juice, and cook for 10 minutes over medium-low heat, stirring occasionally.

In a small mixing bowl combine the cornstarch and water, forming a slurry. When the soup is nearly finished cooking, whisk the slurry into the soup, and simmer for 1 minute, stirring frequently. Stir in the noodles and cilantro, and return to a simmer. Turn off heat and let stand for 5 to 10 minutes, until the noodles are translucent.

Ladle into soup bowls and sprinkle the scallions over the top.

Yield: 3 to 4 servings

Soup Tips

Thai panang curry paste, coconut milk, lemon grass, and cellophane noodles can be found at Asian grocery stores and well-stocked supermarkets. Portobello mushroom caps are available in the produce section of well-stocked supermarkets. If *ketjap manis* is in your pantry, drizzle a little over the soup at the table.

Beet and Pear Borscht

This dramatic fuchsia-hued beet soup is both appetizing and strikingly picturesque. Pears add a soft, fruity nuance and balsamic vinegar offers a hint of well-rounded tanginess.

1	tablespoon canola oil
1	medium yellow onion, diced
2	stalks celery, chopped
2	or 3 cloves garlic, minced
5	cups water
2	cups diced fresh beets (3 or 4 small beets)
2	medium white potatoes, diced (peeled if desired)
1	teaspoon dried thyme
1/2	teaspoon ground black pepper
1/2	teaspoon salt
1/4	teaspoon ground nutmeg
2	firm Bartlett pears, diced
1	to 2 tablespoons balsamic vinegar
2	tablespoons chopped fresh parsley

In a saucepan heat the oil. Add the onion, celery, and garlic, and cook for 5 to 7 minutes over medium heat, stirring frequently. Add the water, beets, potatoes, and dried seasonings, and bring to a simmer. Cook for 40 minutes over medium-low heat, stirring occasionally. Stir in the pears and vinegar, and cook for 15 minutes more until the pears and beets are tender. Stir in the parsley.

Transfer the mixture to a blender or food processor fitted with a steel blade and puree until smooth. Keep hot until ready to serve. As with most beet soups, a swirl of lowfat yogurt or sour cream is a fitting final touch.

Yield: 6 servings

Soup Tips
When the season allows, I like to add 1 or 2 tablespoons of a chopped fresh herb mixture (such as chives, oregano, and parsley) at the finish.

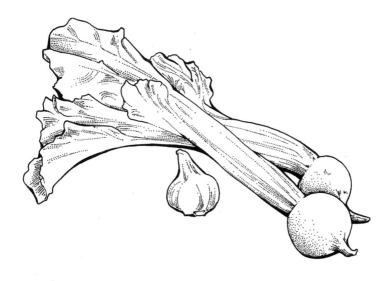

Fifteen Bean Tureen

As beans have grown in popularity, commercially premixed combinations of dried legumes have appeared in the supermarkets and natural food stores. The classic 15-bean mixture contains a wide assortment of legumes, from split peas and lentils to small and large white beans, kidney beans, pinto beans, and others.

1 1/2 cups dried 15-bean mixture, soaked overnight and drained
9   cups water
1   tablespoon canola oil
1   large red onion, diced
1   large green or red bell pepper, seeded and diced
2   stalks celery, diced
2   or 3 cloves garlic, minced
1   (14-ounce) can stewed tomatoes
1   large red or white potato, diced (about 2 cups)
1 1/2 tablespoons Worcestershire sauce
1/4   cup tomato paste
1   tablespoon dried oregano
1   tablespoon chili powder
2   teaspoons ground cumin
1   teaspoon ground black pepper
1   teaspoon salt

In a large saucepan combine the 15-bean mixture and water and bring to a simmer. Cook for about 1½ hours (uncovered) over medium-low heat until the beans are tender, stirring occasionally.

In another large saucepan heat the oil. Add the onion, bell pepper, celery, and garlic; sauté for about 5 to 7 minutes. Stir in the cooked beans, cooking liquid, stewed tomatoes, potato, Worcestershire sauce, tomato paste, and seasonings, and cook for about 30 minutes longer over low heat, stirring occasionally. Remove from the heat, cover the pan, and let stand for 5 to 10 minutes before serving.

Ladle the soup into bowls and serve with warm French or Italian bread.

Yield: 6 to 8 servings

Soup Tips

If you have a wide selection of legumes at home you can make your own 15 bean mixture. Almost any legume can be used, including green and yellow split peas, lentils, white, red, black, pink, and red beans, and black-eyed peas.

Rutabaga and Squash Stew

Rutabagas have a mild, turnip flavor and sturdy texture. They are a welcome ingredient in long-cooking stews and soups and team up well with winter squash. Kale adds a splash of color at the finish.

1	tablespoon canola oil
1	medium yellow onion, diced
2	stalks celery, chopped
1	red bell pepper, seeded and diced
3	or 4 cloves garlic, minced
6	cups water
2	cups peeled and diced butternut squash
2	cups peeled and diced rutabaga
2	to 3 teaspoons dried oregano
1 1/2	teaspoons paprika
1	teaspoon salt
1/2	teaspoon ground black pepper
2	cups chopped kale or red chard
1/4	cup chopped fresh parsley

In a large saucepan heat the oil. Add the onion, celery, bell pepper, and garlic, and sauté for about 5 minutes. Add the water, squash, rutabaga, and dried seasonings, and bring to a simmer. Cook for 40 to 45 minutes over medium-low heat until the rutabaga is tender, stirring occasionally. Stir in the kale and cook for about 10 minutes more.

To thicken, mash the squash and rutabaga against the side of the pan with the back of a spoon. Stir in the parsley and let the stew stand for 5 to 10 minutes before serving.

Ladle into bowls and serve hot.

Yield: 6 to 8 servings

Soup Tips

Other winter squash, such as red kuri, buttercup, or Hubbard, may be substituted for the butternut squash.

Beet Vichyssoise

"This soup is sooo good!" my friends exclaimed upon tasting this raspberry-colored creation. "I love the color!" one of them howled. This velvety combination of humble beets, leeks, and herbs is a feast for the senses.

1	tablespoon canola oil
1	medium yellow onion, diced
2	cups rinsed and chopped leeks
2	cloves garlic, minced
6	cups water
3	cups fresh beets, scrubbed and diced (2 or 3 beets)
2	cups peeled and diced white potatoes
1/4	cup dry red wine
1 1/2	tablespoons dried parsley
1/2	teaspoon ground black pepper
1/2	teaspoon salt
1/4	cup chopped fresh watercress, dill, or parsley
8	ounces lowfat plain yogurt (optional)

In a large saucepan heat the oil. Add the onion, leeks, and garlic, and sauté for 5 to 7 minutes. Add the water, beets, potatoes, wine, and seasonings, and cook for 40 to 45 minutes over low heat, stirring occasionally, until the beets are tender. Set aside and stir in the herbs. Let cool slightly.

Transfer the mixture to a blender or food processor fitted with a steel blade and puree until smooth. Return to the pan and keep hot until ready to serve.

Ladle into bowls and garnish with a sprig of herbs. If you'd like, swirl a dollop of lowfat yogurt in the center of each bowl.

Yield: 6 to 8 servings

Chapter 4

Winter Rhapsodies: Every Day a Soup Day

Where I come from, soup is considered the universal antidote for winter. A bowl of soup cushions the blow of harsh nor'easter winds; soup calms chattering teeth and warms rosy cheeks. The mere aroma of a soup kettle simmering on the stove top brings comfort to down-trodden souls with dripping wet socks. All in all, soup is the venerable cure for the winter blues.

The well-stocked winter pantry makes a multitude of cold-weather cauldrons possible. Wintry soups and stews feature an entourage of colorful legumes such as black, white, and red beans, chickpeas, split peas, lentils, black-eyed peas, and exotic heirloom beans. Grains such as brown rice, white rice, quinoa, and barley provide long lasting energy and substance. A panorama of pastas—tubular tubettini, grain-shaped orzo, small shells, miniature spirals, and others—inspire wonderful soups as well.

Winter soups and stews also rely on hardy "root cellar" vegetables such as potatoes, yams, parsnips, beets, carrots, and winter squash. Although fresh vegetables are often scarce or expensive during winter, versatile canned tomatoes provide welcome flavors and body to soups and stews. Herbs and seasonings from the spice rack provide perky nuances, personality, and character.

The following chapter beckons with alluring soups, hearty stews, and boisterous chilies. From the supremely filling Black Bean Posole and Split Pea and Wild Rice Soup to the salubrious Sunday Supper Soup, Mondo Chili, and Tuscan Country Bean and Escarole Soup, there is a wide and enticing selection of stick-to-your-ribs meals glistening in bowls. In addition, there are healthful and meatless adaptations of wintertime classics such as Red Bean Gumbo Z' Herbes, Tomato Lentil Soup with Orzo, and Root Vegetable Pot-au-Feu. Although it may be cold outside, these enchanted soups and stews will make it feel warm inside.

Black Bean Posole

Posole is a spicy Southwestern chili-stew whose main ingredient is hominy, a kind of chewy, chickpea-shaped dried corn. Hominy adds substance and texture to the soup pot; here it teams up with earthy black beans, aromatic vegetables, and assertive spices.

1	cup dried black beans, soaked overnight and drained
6	cups water
1	tablespoon canola oil
1	medium yellow onion, diced
1	green or red bell pepper, seeded and diced
2	stalks celery, sliced
2	cloves garlic, minced
1	(15-ounce) can crushed tomatoes
1	(14-ounce) can white corn hominy, drained
2	tablespoons minced fresh parsley
2	to 3 teaspoons dried oregano
2	teaspoons ground cumin
1½	teaspoons chili powder
½	teaspoon ground black pepper
½	teaspoon salt

Combine the beans and water in a saucepan and bring to a simmer. Cook for 1 to 1½ hours over low heat, until the beans are tender. Drain, reserving 2 cups of the cooking liquid.

In a large saucepan heat the oil. Add the onion, bell pepper, celery, and garlic, and sauté for about 7 minutes. Stir in the beans, cooking liquid, crushed tomatoes, hominy, and seasonings, and bring to a simmer. Cook for about 20 minutes over medium-low heat, stirring occasionally. Remove from the heat and let stand for 10 minutes before serving.

Ladle the *posole* into bowls and serve hot. Warm flour tortillas make a nice accompaniment.

Yield: 6 servings

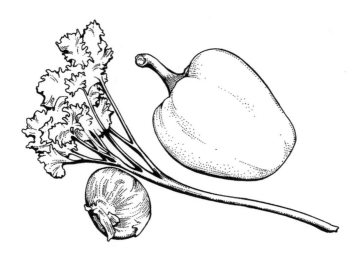

Wintry Tomato Vegetable Soup

This wholesome soup is the proper antidote for the winter blues.

1	tablespoon canola oil or olive oil
1	medium yellow onion, diced
1	small zucchini, diced
8	to 10 mushrooms, sliced
2	large cloves garlic, minced
6	cups water
1	(14-ounce) can stewed tomatoes
1	(6-ounce) can tomato paste
1¹/₂	tablespoons dried parsley
2	teaspoons dried basil
2	teaspoons dried oregano
1	teaspoon salt
¹/₂	teaspoon ground black pepper
¹/₂	cup uncooked tubettini or ditalini pasta
¹/₂	cup shredded part-skim mozzarella or provolone cheese (optional)

In a large saucepan heat the oil. Add the onion, zucchini, mushrooms, and garlic, and sauté for 7 minutes. Add the water, stewed tomatoes, tomato paste, and seasonings, and bring to a simmer. Cook for 15 minutes over medium-low heat, stirring occasionally. Stir in the pasta and cook for 15 to 20 minutes more over low heat until the pasta is al dente. Occasionally stir the soup while it cooks.

Let the soup sit for 10 minutes before serving. Ladle into bowls and, if desired, top with shredded cheese. Serve with warm Italian bread.

Yield: 6 to 8 servings

Moroccan Lentil and Kale Stew

This satisfying cauldron of lentils, carrots, and kale will satisfy almost any hungry appetite. In the spirit of traditional Moroccan soups, this version calls for a last-minute spritz of fresh lemon and a topping of golden sautéed onions.

1	tablespoon canola oil
2	large carrots, peeled and diced
1	medium yellow onion, diced
2	cloves garlic, minced
7	cups water
1 1/2	cups green or red lentils, rinsed
2	teaspoons ground cumin
1/2	teaspoon ground black pepper
2	cups coarsely chopped kale
3	or 4 tablespoons chopped fresh parsley
1	teaspoon salt
	Juice of 1 lemon
2	teaspoons olive oil
1	large yellow onion, thinly sliced

In a large saucepan heat the canola oil. Add the carrots, diced onion, and garlic, and sauté for 5 minutes. Stir in the water, lentils, cumin, and pepper, and bring to a simmer. Cook over low heat for 45 to 55 minutes, stirring occasionally, until the lentils are tender. Stir in the kale, parsley, salt, and lemon juice, and cook for 10 minutes more.

Meanwhile, heat the olive oil in a skillet. Add the sliced onion and sauté for 5 to 7 minutes, until lightly browned.

Ladle the soup into bowls and top each serving with a portion of the browned onions.

Yield: 6 to 8 servings

Spanish Chickpea and Garlic Soup

Chickpeas and garlic find their way into a variety of enticing Spanish soups. Although chickpeas take longer to cook than most legumes, one's patience is aptly rewarded once this amber-hued broth is ladled into the bowl.

1 1/2	cups dried chickpeas, soaked overnight and drained
10	cups water
1	tablespoon olive oil
1	medium yellow onion, diced
4	cloves garlic, minced
1	large tomato, diced
4	scallions, chopped
2	medium carrots, peeled and diced
2	cups white potatoes, coarsely chopped (peeled if desired)
1	teaspoon paprika
1/2	teaspoon ground black pepper
1/2	teaspoon salt
2	to 3 tablespoons chopped fresh parsley

In a large saucepan combine the chickpeas and water. Bring to a simmer and cook for about 1½ to 2 hours over low heat, until the peas are tender. Drain the peas, reserving 5 cups of the cooking liquid. (Add water if there is less liquid than the amount required.)

In another large saucepan heat the oil. Add the onion and garlic, and sauté for 4 minutes. Add the tomato, scallions, and carrots, and sauté for 1 minute more. Stir in the chickpeas, cooking liquid, potatoes, and dried seasonings, and bring to a simmer. Cook for 30 to 40 minutes over medium-low heat, stirring occasionally.

Remove from the heat and stir in the parsley. If you prefer a creamy soup, transfer half (or all) of the soup to a blender or food processor fitted with a steel blade and puree until smooth. Return to the pan and keep hot until ready to serve.

Serve as a chunky soup with warm bread.

Yield: 6 to 8 servings

Beet Gumbo

This is a beet lover's delight. Beets produce an inviting cranberry-hued gumbo; brown rice adds substance and body. Beet greens added at the last minute contribute zest and vitality.

1	tablespoon canola oil
1	medium yellow onion, diced
1	green bell pepper, seeded and diced
2	stalks celery, sliced
2	or 3 cloves garlic, minced
6	cups hot water
2	cups diced and peeled beets
1	(14-ounce) can stewed tomatoes
1/2	cup long grain brown rice
1	teaspoon Tabasco or other bottled hot sauce
2	teaspoons dried oregano
1	teaspoon dried thyme
1	teaspoon salt
1/2	teaspoon ground black pepper
2	cups coarsely chopped beet greens or spinach
3	to 4 tablespoons chopped fresh parsley

In a large saucepan heat the oil. Add the onion, bell pepper, celery, and garlic, and cook for 7 to 9 minutes over medium heat, stirring frequently. Stir in the water, beets, stewed tomatoes, rice, Tabasco, and dried seasonings.

Cook over low heat for 50 minutes to 1 hour, stirring occasionally, until the beets are tender. Stir in the beet greens and parsley, and cook for 5 to 10 minutes more.

Let the gumbo stand for 10 to 15 minutes before serving. Serve with warm bread or corn bread.

Yield: 6 to 8 servings

Soup Tips

Look for beet roots with their leafy tops still attached. The greens add valuable nutrients and flavor.

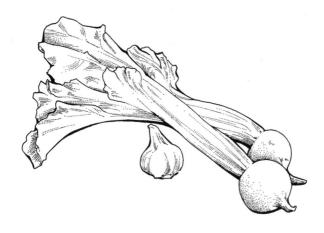

Triple Pepper Chili

A steaming bowl of meatless chili beckons with wholesome satisfaction; it tastes good, looks good, and it is good for you. This piquant chili resonates with a trio of chile peppers: ancho, bell pepper, and jalapeño. Ancho chiles are dried, anvil-shaped poblano chiles with a husky, raisiny heat.

1	or 2 ancho chiles
2	teaspoons canola oil
1	medium yellow onion, diced
1	red bell pepper, seeded and diced
1	large stalk celery, chopped
2	or 3 cloves garlic, minced
1	jalapeño pepper, seeded and minced
2	(15-ounce) cans black beans or red kidney beans, drained
1	(28-ounce) can crushed tomatoes
1	tablespoon chopped fresh parsley
1	tablespoon chili powder
2	teaspoons dried oregano
1/2	teaspoon salt

Soak the ancho chiles in enough warm water to cover for 30 minutes to 1 hour. Drain; remove the seeds and chop the chiles.

In a large saucepan heat the oil. Add the onion, bell pepper, celery, garlic, and jalapeño, and cook for about 7 minutes over medium heat, stirring frequently, until the vegetables are tender. Add the beans, crushed tomatoes, and seasonings, and bring to a simmer. Cook for 15 to 20 minutes over low heat, stirring occasionally.

Ladle the chili into bowls and serve with warm bread or Quintessential Corn Bread (page 239).

Yield: 4 servings

Soup Tips
If ancho chiles are unavailable, try 1 chipotle chile or guajillo chile.

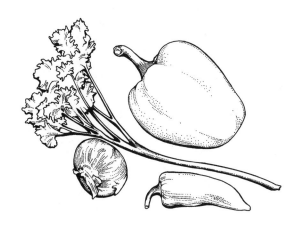

Red Lentil Mulligatawny

Mulligatawny is a peppery Indian soup with a hint of fruitiness. Red lentils dissolve quickly into the cooking liquid and yield an earthy, hearty broth. Like Cajun gumbo, mulligatawny is traditionally served with rice. Fragrant basmati rice makes a natural accompaniment.

3/4	cup red lentils
6	to 8 cups water
1	tablespoon canola oil
1	medium yellow onion, diced
2	cloves garlic, minced
2	teaspoons minced fresh ginger
1	large tomato, diced
2 1/2	teaspoons curry powder
1 1/2	teaspoons ground cumin
1/2	teaspoon garam masala
1	teaspoon salt
1/4	teaspoon ground cayenne pepper
1	large white potato, diced (peeled if desired)
1	large carrot, peeled and diced
1/2	cup raisins
2	small unpeeled red apples, diced
4	to 6 cups cooked white or brown rice, preferably basmati

In a medium saucepan combine the lentils and water. Bring to a simmer and cook for 30 minutes over low-medium heat, stirring occasionally.

In a large saucepan heat the oil. Add the onion, garlic, and ginger, and sauté for 3 to 4 minutes. Add the tomato and seasonings, and sauté for 1 minute more. Stir in the lentils, cooking liquid, potato, carrot, and raisins, and cook over medium-low heat for about 20 minutes until the lentils are tender, stirring occasionally. Stir in the apples and cook for 10 minutes more. Let stand for 5 to 10 minutes before serving.

Spoon the rice into soup bowls and ladle the mulligatawny over the top. Serve with warm Indian flat bread or pita bread.

Yield: 6 to 8 servings

Soup Tips

Look for red lentils in natural food stores and well-stocked supermarkets. Green or brown lentils may be substituted, but plan to cook them about ten to fifteen minutes longer.

Black Bean Chili
with Salsa Mexicana

From the moment I first tasted a black bean chili at a trendy San Francisco restaurant, I have been hooked. It was a brilliant idea—why hadn't I thought of it before? This meatless version is accompanied by fresh Mexican salsa (also called pico de gallo).

For the salsa:

2	medium tomatoes, diced
1	small red onion, chopped
1	jalapeño or serrano chile, seeded and minced
2	tablespoons chopped cilantro
	Juice of 1 lime

For the chili:

2	teaspoons canola oil
1	medium yellow onion, diced
1	green or red bell pepper, seeded and diced
2	stalks celery, chopped
2	or 3 cloves garlic, minced
2	(15-ounce) cans black beans, drained
1	(28-ounce) can crushed tomatoes
1½	tablespoons dried parsley
1	tablespoon chili powder
2	teaspoons dried oregano
1½	to 2 teaspoons ground cumin
½	teaspoon salt

In a medium mixing bowl combine the tomatoes, onion, jalapeño, cilantro, and lime juice. Refrigerate for 1 hour. (The salsa can be made up to a day in advance.)

In a large saucepan heat the oil. Add the onion, bell pepper, celery, and garlic, and sauté for 5 to 7 minutes over medium heat, until the vegetables are tender. Add the beans, crushed tomatoes, and seasonings. Bring to a simmer and cook for 15 to 20 minutes over low heat, stirring occasionally.

Ladle the chili into bowls and top with the salsa. Serve with warm flour tortillas or cheese bread on the side.

Yield: 4 to 6 servings

Caribbean Red Pea Soup

While traveling throughout the Caribbean, I have savored a variety of nourishing bean soups. Jamaica is famous for its red pea soup (kidney beans are called red peas); Barbados is home to gungo pea soup, a similar creation. This version includes whole scallions, thyme branches, Scotch bonnet peppers, and an island touch of coconut and allspice.

1 1/2 cups dried red kidney beans, soaked overnight and drained
10   cups water
1   tablespoon canola oil
1   large yellow onion, diced
1   large bell pepper, seeded and diced
3   or 4 cloves garlic, minced
3   or 4 whole scallions
1   whole Scotch bonnet pepper, punctured with a fork (optional)
1   large sweet potato, diced (do not peel)
4   or 5 thyme branches (or 1 1/2 teaspoons dried thyme)
1   cup canned lowfat coconut milk
2   tablespoons dried parsley
1/2   teaspoon ground black pepper
1/2   teaspoon ground allspice
1   teaspoon salt

In a large saucepan combine the beans and water. Bring to a simmer and cook over low heat for 1 to 1½ hours until tender. Drain and reserve 5½ cups of the cooking liquid.

In another large saucepan heat the oil. Add the onion, bell pepper, and garlic, and sauté for 5 to 7 minutes. Add the beans, cooking liquid, and all of the remaining ingredients except the salt. Bring to a simmer and cook for 1 hour over medium-low heat, stirring occasionally. Remove the Scotch bonnet after 30 or 40 minutes. (The longer you leave it in, the spicier the soup will be.) Save the chile for a brave soul at the table.

Before serving, remove the thyme branches and stir in the salt. To thicken, ladle half (or all) of the soup into a blender or food processor fitted with a steel blade; puree for about 10 seconds. Return to the pan and keep hot until ready to serve.

Yield: 8 to 10 servings

Soup Tips

Red pea soup can also include carrots, potatoes, West Indian pumpkin, spinach, or whatever is in season. Fiery Scotch bonnet peppers are available in the produce section of well-stocked supermarkets and in Caribbean grocery stores.

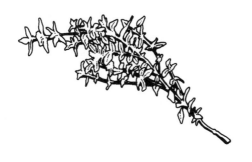

Split Pea and Wild Rice Soup

The secret to cooking split peas is patience. Split peas cannot be rushed; they take their own sweet time. Here the lazy legumes are complemented with wild rice, the dark, slender grains native to Minnesota and Canada. The striking combination offers a cauldron of inviting textures and nutty flavors. This is a soup to sink your teeth into.

1	tablespoon canola oil
1	large red onion, diced
2	stalks celery, chopped
2	or 3 cloves garlic, minced
10	cups water
1	cup green split peas, soaked for 2 hours and drained
2	large carrots, peeled and diced
1	large white potato, diced (peeled if desired)
1/2	cup wild rice
2	tablespoons dried parsley
2	teaspoons oregano
3/4	teaspoon ground black pepper
1	teaspoon salt

In a large saucepan heat the oil. Add the onion, celery, and garlic, and sauté for 5 minutes. Stir in the water, split peas, carrots, potato, wild rice, and seasonings (except the salt), and cook for 1½ to 2 hours over medium-low heat, stirring occasionally.

Stir in the salt and cook for 5 to 10 minutes more over low heat.

Ladle the soup into bowls and serve with hearth-style bread.

Yield: 6 to 8 servings

Soup Tips

Wild rice is available in the grain sections of natural food stores and well-stocked supermarkets.

Sicilian Pasta
and Chickpea Soup

Chickpeas, called ceci beans (pronounced cheh-chee) in Italian, are complemented by tiny pasta shells perfect for soup. Each spoonful holds the chickpeas and soup shells nestled together. A last-minute addition of kale supplies vivid colors and valuable nutrients. My Sicilian-American mother contributed this recipe.

1	tablespoon olive oil
1	medium yellow onion, diced
2	cups diced zucchini
2	or 3 cloves garlic, minced
8	cups hot water
1	(14-ounce) can stewed tomatoes
2	cups diced white potatoes
1/4	cup tomato paste
2	teaspoons dried oregano
1	teaspoon dried basil
1	teaspoon salt
1/2	teaspoon ground black pepper
1/2	cup small soup shells or spirals
1	(15-ounce) can chickpeas, drained
2	cups coarsely chopped kale or red chard
2	tablespoons chopped fresh parsley

In a large saucepan heat the oil. Add the onion, zucchini, and garlic, and sauté for 5 minutes. Stir in the water, stewed tomatoes, potatoes, tomato paste, and dried seasonings, and bring to a simmer. Cook for about 20 minutes over medium-low heat, stirring occasionally.

Stir in the pasta, chickpeas, kale, and parsley, and cook for 10 to 12 minutes more, stirring frequently. Set aside for 10 minutes before serving.

Ladle the soup into bowls and serve with warm Italian bread.

Yield: 8 servings

Soup Tips

I like to sprinkle this soup with pecorino Romano cheese, which has a slightly stronger flavor than Parmesan. If fresh basil is available, add 2 or 3 tablespoons (chopped) to the soup at the last minute. If you have the chance, add purple basil.

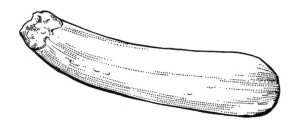

Tuscan Country Bean and Escarole Soup

A cup of this soup runneth over with vegetables, beans, herbs, and escarole, a wide leafy green with a mildly bitter flavor. When this minestrone-style soup is served over bread the next day, it is called ribollita (Italian for "reboiled").

1	tablespoon olive oil
1	medium yellow onion, diced
2	cups rinsed and chopped leeks
3	or 4 cloves garlic, minced
6	cups hot water
1	(28-ounce) can whole tomatoes
2	cups diced white potatoes (peeled if desired)
2	medium carrots, peeled and diced
1/4	cup tomato paste
1 1/2	tablespoons dried parsley (or 3 tablespoons fresh parsley, chopped)
2	teaspoons dried oregano
1	teaspoon salt
1/2	teaspoon ground sage
1/2	teaspoon ground black pepper
1	(15-ounce) can white kidney beans (cannellini), drained
2	cups coarsely chopped escarole or kale
1/2	cup grated Romano or Parmesan cheese (optional)

In a large saucepan heat the oil. Add the onion, leeks, and garlic, and sauté for 5 minutes. Stir in the water, tomatoes, potatoes, carrots, tomato paste, and seasonings, and bring to a simmer. Cook for 20 to 25 minutes over medium-low heat, stirring occasionally.

Stir in the beans and escarole and cook for 10 to 15 minutes more, stirring frequently. Set aside for 10 minutes before serving.

Ladle the soup into bowls and serve with warm Tuscan-style bread. If desired, sprinkle the cheese over the top.

Yield: 8 servings

Southwestern Posole Chili

Posole is a Southwestern stew of hominy (dried corn), vegetables, and spices. Here posole merges with a Tex-Mex "bowl of red," or chili. The result is a serious bowl of wholesome goodness.

1   tablespoon canola oil
1   medium yellow onion, diced
1   large red or green bell pepper, seeded and diced
2   cloves garlic, minced
1   (28-ounce) can crushed tomatoes
1   (15-ounce) can hominy, drained
1   (15-ounce) can red kidney beans, drained
1   (14-ounce) can stewed tomatoes
1/2 cup water
1   tablespoon dried oregano
2   to 3 teaspoons chili powder
2   teaspoons ground cumin
1/2 teaspoon ground black pepper
1/2 teaspoon salt
2   tablespoons chopped cilantro

In a large saucepan heat the oil. Add the onion, bell pepper, and garlic, and sauté for about 5 minutes. Stir in the crushed tomatoes, hominy, beans, tomatoes, water, and seasonings (except the cilantro). Cook for 25 to 30 minutes over low heat, stirring occasionally.

Remove from the heat and stir in the cilantro. Let stand for 5 to 10 minutes before serving. Offer warm flour tortillas on the side.

Yield: 6 servings

Soup Tips

I like to offer a selection of toppings such as chopped scallions, jalapeño peppers, and shredded lowfat cheddar cheese. Hominy is available canned or frozen in most well-stocked grocery stores. (If using dried hominy, cook it for about three hours before adding to the *posole.)*

Tomato Zuppa
with Herb Croutons

This is the winter version of Pappa al Pomodoro, a classic Italian tomato and bread soup (page 232). The garlic-scented tomato bisque is ladled over croutons and allowed to soak and mingle. It is quick, easy to prepare, and delicioso.

4	to 6 slices firm-textured dark bread or Italian bread, cut into 1/2-inch cubes
1	tablespoon mixture of dried oregano, basil, and thyme
1	tablespoon olive oil
1	medium yellow onion, diced
3	or 4 cloves garlic, minced
1	(28-ounce) can stewed tomatoes
2	cups hot water
2	teaspoons dried oregano
2	teaspoons dried parsley
1/2	teaspoon salt
1/2	teaspoon ground black pepper
	About 1/4 cup grated Parmesan or Romano cheese (optional)

In a mixing bowl toss the bread cubes with the herb mixture. Spread the cubes out on a baking pan lined with wax paper. Place in the oven and broil for 5 to 10 minutes (or bake at 375°) until lightly toasted. Set aside and let cool.

In a large saucepan heat the oil. Add the onion and garlic, and sauté for 4 minutes. Stir in the stewed tomatoes, water, and seasonings, and bring to a simmer. Cook for about 20 minutes over medium-low heat, stirring occasionally.

Remove from the heat and let cool slightly. Transfer the soup to a blender or food processor fitted with a steel blade and process for about 10 seconds until pureed. Return to the pan.

Place 3 or 4 croutons in the bottom of each soup bowl. Ladle the soup over the top. Gently pack the soup and croutons together. If desired, sprinkle a little Parmesan or Romano cheese over the top.

Yield: 4 servings

Soup Tips

If available, add about 2 tablespoons chopped basil, parsley, or arugula to the soup before pureeing.

Red Bean Gumbo Z' Herbes

When it comes to gumbo, anything goes. During the Lenten season, meatless gumbo z' herbes is popular, and a multitude of leafy greens and beans replaces the traditional meat and seafood. It is said that for each kind of green added to the gumbo, you will make a new friend.

1	tablespoon canola oil
1	medium yellow onion, diced
1	green or red bell pepper, seeded and diced
1	stalk celery, chopped
2	or 3 cloves garlic, minced
6	cups water or vegetable stock
1	(14-ounce) can stewed tomatoes
1/4	cup tomato paste
1 1/2	teaspoons dried oregano
1	teaspoon dried thyme
1/2	teaspoon ground black pepper
1/2	teaspoon ground cayenne pepper
1/2	teaspoon salt
4	cups chopped mixed greens (such as spinach, mustard greens, kale, or dandelion greens)
1	(15-ounce) can red kidney beans, drained
2	to 3 tablespoons chopped fresh parsley
3	to 4 cups cooked wild pecan rice or basmati rice

In a large saucepan heat the oil. Add the onion, bell pepper, celery, and garlic, and sauté for 5 to 7 minutes. Stir in the water, stewed tomatoes, tomato paste, and dried seasonings, and bring to a simmer. Cook over medium-low heat for 15 minutes, stirring occasionally. Stir in the mixed greens and beans, and cook for about 10 minutes more. Stir in the parsley and remove from the heat.

When ready to serve, place about 1/2 cup cooked rice in the bottom of each soup bowl. Ladle the gumbo over the rice.

Yield: 6 to 8 servings

Soup Tips

Gumbo is almost always served over (or with) rice. Wild Pecan rice is a rice grown in Louisiana, but any fragrant rice, such as basmati, jasmine, or American Texmati, can be used.

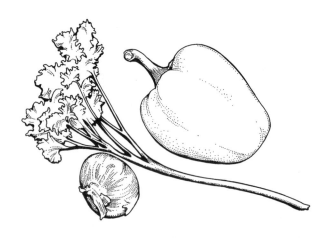

Curried Spinach and Potato Stew

This warm, wholesome soup is infused with curry spices and chiles. A welcome heat wave washes across the taste buds.

1	tablespoon canola oil
1	medium yellow onion, diced
2	cloves garlic, minced
1	or 2 jalapeño or other hot chiles, seeded and minced
2	teaspoons curry powder
1	teaspoon ground cumin
1/2	teaspoon salt
1/4	teaspoon cayenne pepper
1/4	teaspoon ground turmeric
4	cups water or vegetable stock
1	(14-ounce) can stewed tomatoes
2	cups diced white potatoes (peeled if desired)
2	medium carrots, peeled and diced
1	(10-ounce) package frozen chopped spinach

In a large saucepan heat the oil. Add the onion, garlic, and jalapeño, and sauté for 4 minutes. Stir in the seasonings and cook for 1 minute more. Stir in the water, stewed tomatoes, potatoes, and carrots, and bring to a simmer. Cook over medium-low heat for 20 minutes, stirring occasionally. Stir in the spinach and cook for about 15 minutes more over low heat, stirring occasionally. Let stand for 5 to 10 minutes before serving. To thicken, mash some of the potatoes against the side of the pan with the back of a large spoon.

Ladle into bowls and serve with warm Indian flat bread or Skillet Roti Bread (page 249).

Yield: 6 servings

Soup Tips

For a cooling condiment, serve lowfat plain yogurt or Cucumber Yogurt Raita (page 241) on the side.

Root Vegetable Pot-au-Feu

This pot-au-feu captures the rugged spirit of hardy root veg-
etables. After turnips, parsnips, carrots, and leeks simmer
for a while, a kind of alchemy takes place. Pot au feu means
"pot over fire" in French. A touch of tarragon brings out
memories of anise and licorice.

1	tablespoon canola oil
1	medium yellow onion, diced
1	cup leeks, rinsed and chopped
1	large stalk celery, chopped
2	or 3 cloves garlic, minced
6	cups water or vegetable stock
2	medium carrots, peeled and diced
1	medium parsnip or white potato, peeled and diced
1	medium turnip, peeled and diced
2	tablespoons dry white wine
1	tablespoon dried parsley (or 2 tablespoons chopped fresh parsley)
1	teaspoon dried tarragon or Herbes de Provence
3/4	teaspoon salt
1/2	teaspoon ground black pepper

In a large saucepan heat the oil. Add the onion, leeks, celery, and garlic, and sauté for about 5 minutes. Add the water, carrots, parsnip or potato, turnip, wine, and seasonings, and bring to a simmer. Cook for 40 to 50 minutes over low heat, stirring occasionally, until the vegetables are tender.

Let the soup stand for 5 to 10 minutes before serving. Ladle into bowls and serve with warm dark bread or French bread.

Yield: 6 servings

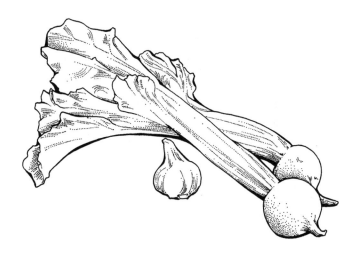

South American Quinoa and Corn Soup

Quinoa is an ancient grain grown in the altiplano (highlands) of South America. The Incas called quinoa the "mother grain," and in fact it has a mother lode of protein and other nutrients. For this soup the tiny ringlike grain is combined with corn, tomatoes, peppers, and beans.

1	tablespoon canola oil
1	medium yellow onion, diced
1	red or green bell pepper, seeded and diced
1	celery stalk, chopped
2	cloves garlic, minced
1	jalapeño pepper, seeded and minced (optional)
2	medium tomatoes, diced
1 1/2	tablespoons dried parsley
2	teaspoons paprika
2	teaspoons dried oregano
3/4	teaspoon salt
1/2	teaspoon ground black pepper
6	cups water
1/2	cup quinoa, rinsed
2	cups corn kernels, fresh or frozen
1	(15-ounce) can chickpeas or red kidney beans, drained

In a large saucepan heat the oil. Add the onion, bell pepper, celery, garlic, and jalapeño, and sauté for about 5 minutes. Add the tomatoes and seasonings, and sauté for 3 to 4 minutes more, until the mixture forms a thick pulp.

Add the water, quinoa, and corn, and cook for 25 minutes over medium-low heat, stirring occasionally. Stir in the beans and cook for about 5 minutes more.

Let the soup stand for 10 minutes before serving.

Yield: 6 servings

Soup Tips

Look for quinoa in natural food stores and well-stocked grocery stores. Before cooking quinoa, it is important to rinse it to wash away a natural, bitter-tasting resin that coats the grains.

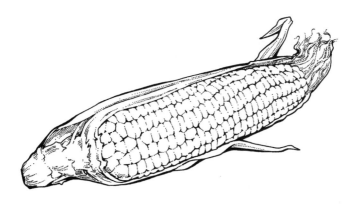

Sun-Dried Tomato Risotto Soup

In the winter months sun-dried tomatoes provide a temporary reprieve from the squarish, bland tomatoes on the market. Arborio rice, the grain that gives risotto its signature creaminess, gives this soup a similar body and texture.

1	cup sun-dried tomatoes
2	cups warm water
1	tablespoon canola oil
1	medium red onion, diced
1	large celery stalk, chopped
2	or 3 cloves garlic, minced
5	cups water
1/2	cup arborio rice or other short grain white rice
1/4	cup dry white wine
1	teaspoon dried basil
1/2	teaspoon salt
1/2	teaspoon ground white pepper
1/3	pound fresh green beans, trimmed and cut into 1-inch pieces
2	to 3 tablespoons chopped fresh basil or parsley (optional)
1/3	to 1/2 cup grated Parmesan or Romano cheese

Cover the dried tomatoes in the water and soak for 30 minutes to 1 hour. Drain, reserving the liquid. Coarsely chop the tomatoes.

In a large saucepan heat the oil. Add the onion, celery, and garlic, and sauté for 5 to 7 minutes. Add the tomatoes, soaking liquid, water, rice, wine, and dried seasonings, and cook over low-medium heat for 20 minutes, stirring occasionally. Stir in the green beans and cook for 10 minutes more over low heat.

Remove from the heat and blend in the fresh herbs and cheese. Ladle the soup into bowls and serve with warm Italian bread. Pass any extra cheese at the table.

Yield: 6 servings

Soup Tips

Arborio rice can be found in gourmet grocery stores and well-stocked supermarkets.

Red Cabbage Borscht

Mention borscht to some people and they might recall fond memories of borschts past; others might squinch up their face with a look of mock horror. The first time I tasted a borscht, it was not love at first bite. But in the hands of the right chef, borscht comes alive with savory flavors. This healthful combination of red cabbage, beets, carrot, and potato proves the point.

1	tablespoon canola oil
1	medium yellow onion, diced
1	stalk celery, sliced
2	cloves garlic, minced
6 1/2	cups water
2	medium beets, scrubbed and diced
2	cups coarsely chopped red cabbage
1	large white or sweet potato, diced (peeled if desired)
1	large carrot, peeled and diced
1/4	cup dry red wine
1 1/2	tablespoons dried parsley
1	teaspoon dried thyme
1/2	teaspoon ground black pepper
1/2	teaspoon salt
3	to 4 tablespoons chopped fresh chives, parsley, or dill (for garnish)
8	ounces lowfat plain yogurt (optional)

In a large saucepan heat the oil. Add the onion, celery, and garlic, and sauté for 5 minutes. Add the water, beets, cabbage, potato, carrot, wine, and dried seasonings, and cook for 45 to 50 minutes over low heat, stirring occasionally until the vegetables are tender. Set aside and let cool slightly.

Transfer the mixture to a blender or food processor fitted with a steel blade and puree until smooth. Return to the pan and keep hot until ready to serve, or chill for later. (Borscht can be served hot or cold, depending on the season.)

Ladle the borscht into bowls and sprinkle the fresh herbs over the top. If you'd like, swirl a dollop of yogurt in the center of each bowl.

Yield: 6 to 8 servings

Wild Rice, Sweet Potato, and Corn Chowder

This soup is "Made in America": the wild rice hails from Minnesota, sweet potatoes come from Louisiana, Vidalia onions grow in Georgia, chiles flourish in the Southwest, and corn is harvested from the nation's heartland. It probably is a good soup to serve on the Fourth of July or Flag Day.

1	tablespoon canola oil
1	medium Vidalia sweet onion or other onion, diced
1	green bell pepper, seeded and diced
2	cloves garlic, minced
1	jalapeño pepper, seeded and minced
6	cups water
1/2	cup wild rice
1 1/2	tablespoons dried parsley
2	teaspoons dried oregano
1	teaspoon ground cumin
3/4	teaspoon salt
1/2	teaspoon ground black pepper
2	cups diced sweet potatoes (peeled if desired)
1 1/2	cups corn kernels, fresh or frozen

In a large saucepan heat the oil. Add the onion, bell pepper, garlic, and jalapeño pepper, and sauté for 5 minutes. Add the water, wild rice, and seasonings, and bring to a simmer. Cook for 20 minutes over medium heat, stirring occasionally. Stir in the sweet potatoes and corn, and cook for 25 to 30 minutes more over low heat, stirring occasionally. Set aside for 10 minutes before serving.

Ladle the soup into bowls and serve with warm flour tortillas or bread.

Yield: 6 servings

Soup Tips

If wild rice is unavailable, try Texmati rice (from Texas) or Wehani rice (from California).

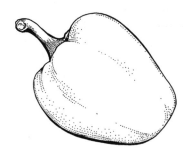

Colorado Anasazi Bean Chili

While visiting my sister in Colorado, I created this cauldron of roasted poblano chiles, Anasazi beans, and aromatic herbs. Anasazi beans are heirloom legumes native to Colorado and named after the Anasazi Indians. The speckled beans were once hard to find but have recently become available at well-stocked natural food stores and specialty markets.

1	cup dried Anasazi beans, soaked overnight and drained
8	cups water
2	poblano or New Mexico chiles
1	tablespoon canola oil
1	medium yellow onion, diced
1	green bell pepper, seeded and diced
1	stalk celery, chopped
2	or 3 cloves garlic, minced
2	large ripe tomatoes, diced
1	(28-ounce) can crushed tomatoes
2	to 3 tablespoons chopped fresh parsley
1	tablespoon chili powder
2	teaspoons dried oregano
1	teaspoon paprika
1/2	teaspoon salt

In a large saucepan combine the beans and water. Bring to a simmer and cook over medium-low heat for 1 to 1 1/2 hours until tender. Drain, discarding the cooking liquid.

Meanwhile, roast the chiles over a hot grill or beneath a broiler until the outside skins are charred. Let cool slightly before peeling and removing the blackened skins. Remove the seeds and chop the chiles.

In a large saucepan heat the oil. Add the onion, bell pepper, celery, and garlic, and sauté for 4 minutes. Stir in the roasted chiles and tomatoes, and cook for 3 to 4 minutes more over medium heat, stirring frequently. Stir in the beans, crushed tomatoes, and seasonings, and cook for 20 minutes over medium-low heat, stirring occasionally. Let stand for 5 to 10 minutes before serving.

Ladle into bowls and serve with Chipotle Corn Bread (page 240) or warm loaf bread.

Yield: 6 servings

Soup Tips

Sprinkle a little shredded Monterey Jack cheese over the top before serving. New Mexico chiles, which are available on a seasonal basis, may be substituted for poblanos.

Southern Black-Eyed Pea and Collard Greens Stew

This wholesome stew combines the hardy staples of the Southern kitchen: black-eyed peas, collard greens, turnips, and potatoes. I like to serve it gumbo-style—over a steaming bowl of rice. It beckons with reassuring comfort on a rainy day.

1	cup black-eyed peas, soaked overnight and drained
8	cups water
1	tablespoon canola oil
1	medium yellow onion, diced
1	stalk celery, chopped
2	or 3 cloves garlic, minced
4	cups coarsely chopped collard greens (chiffonade style)
2	medium carrots, peeled and diced
2	medium turnips, peeled and diced
1	large white potato or sweet potato, diced (peeled if desired)
2	teaspoons dried oregano
1	teaspoon salt
1/2	teaspoon ground black pepper
1/4	cup chopped fresh parsley (or 1 1/2 tablespoons dried)

In a large saucepan combine the peas and water. Bring to a simmer and cook over medium-low heat for 1 to 1½ hours until tender. Drain, reserving 6 cups of the cooking liquid. (Add water if there is less than 6 cups.)

In a large saucepan heat the oil. Add the onion, celery, and garlic, and sauté for about 5 minutes. Add the beans, cooking liquid, collards, carrots, turnips, potato, and dried seasonings, and bring to a simmer. Cook for 35 to 45 minutes over medium-low heat, stirring occasionally, until the vegetables are tender. Stir in the parsley and let stand for 10 minutes before serving.

Ladle into bowls and serve with warm bread and (if desired) a pot of cooked rice.

Yield: 6 to 8 servings

Tomato Tortellini Soup

One of the first soups I ever scribbled down (many years ago) was a version of this tomato vegetable soup with cheese tortellini. The recipe has evolved over the years but continues to be a delicious appetite quencher as well as a sentimental favorite.

1	tablespoon olive oil
1	medium yellow onion, diced
1	small zucchini, diced
10	to 12 mushrooms, sliced
3	or 4 cloves garlic, minced
7	cups water
1	(14-ounce) can stewed tomatoes (or 2 large tomatoes, diced)
1/4	cup dry red wine
1/4	cup canned tomato paste
1	tablespoon dried oregano
2	teaspoons dried basil
1	teaspoon salt
1/4	teaspoon red pepper flakes
6	ounces frozen cheese tortellini or potato gnocchi
1	(15-ounce) can white kidney beans or Roman beans, drained
1/4	pound green beans, trimmed and cut into 1-inch pieces

In a large saucepan heat the oil. Add the onion, zucchini, mushrooms, and garlic, and cook for 7 to 9 minutes over medium heat, stirring frequently. Add the water, tomatoes, wine, tomato paste, and seasonings, and bring to a simmer. Cook for 20 to 25 minutes over medium-low heat, stirring occasionally.

Stir in the pasta, white beans, and green beans, and simmer for 10 to 15 minutes more, until the pasta is al dente. Occasionally stir the soup while it cooks.

Let the soup sit for 10 minutes before serving. Serve with warm Italian bread. Poblano Rouille (page 238) or Garden Forest Pesto (page 248) make enticing toppings.

Yield: 8 servings

Soup Tips

For an herbal nuance, add 2 or 3 tablespoons of chopped fresh basil, oregano, or arugula to the soup at the finish. Also, 2 cups of chopped escarole or kale can be added about 10 minutes before the end.

Pureed Root Soup

For years root vegetables were overlooked or ignored, but recently they have come into vogue. When it comes to soup, they are right at home.

1	tablespoon canola oil
1	medium yellow onion, diced
2	cups rinsed and chopped leeks
2	cloves garlic, minced
4	cups water
2	cups peeled and diced parsnips
2	cups peeled and diced rutabagas or turnips
1/4	cup dry white wine
1 1/2	tablespoons dried parsley
1	teaspoon salt
1/2	teaspoon ground white pepper
2	cups lowfat milk or soy milk
1	tablespoon lemon juice or white wine vinegar
1/4	cup chopped scallions (for garnish)

In a large saucepan heat the oil. Add the onion, leeks, and garlic, and sauté for 5 to 7 minutes. Add the water, parsnips, rutabagas or turnips, white wine, and dried seasonings, and bring to a simmer. Cook over medium-low heat for about 45 minutes to 1 hour, stirring occasionally. Stir in the milk and return to a gentle simmer. Remove from the heat and let cool for a few minutes. Stir in the lemon juice or vinegar.

Transfer the soup to a blender or food processor fitted with a steel blade and puree until smooth. Ladle into bowls and sprinkle the scallions over the top.

Yield: 8 servings

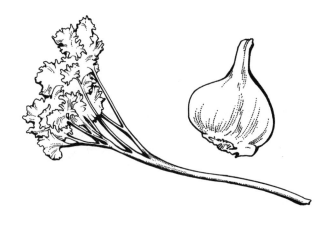

Pasta e Fagioli

What would a soup cookbook be without pasta e fagioli? This classic Italian soup (pronounced pasta fazool) is laden with pasta, vegetables, and beans. It is a wholesome, close-to-the-earth soup meant to be slurped and enjoyed, not eaten with pinkies raised. "Pasta fazool" is one of my favorites. Mumma mia!

1	tablespoon olive oil
1	medium yellow onion, diced
1	small yellow summer squash or zucchini, diced
10	to 12 mushrooms, sliced
3	or 4 cloves garlic, minced
7	cups water
1	(14-ounce) can stewed tomatoes (or 2 large tomatoes, diced)
1/4	cup dry red wine
4	to 6 tablespoons canned tomato paste
1	tablespoon dried oregano
2	teaspoons dried basil
1	teaspoon salt
1/2	teaspoon ground black pepper
1/2	cup ditalini, tubettini, or soup shells
1	(15-ounce) can cannellini beans or Roman beans, drained
1/4	pound green beans, trimmed and cut into 1-inch pieces
1/2	cup grated Parmesan cheese (for garnish)

In a large saucepan heat the oil. Add the onion, zucchini, mushrooms, and garlic, and cook for 7 to 9 minutes over medium heat, stirring frequently. Add the water, tomatoes, wine, tomato paste, and seasonings, and bring to a simmer. Cook for 20 to 25 minutes over medium-low heat, stirring occasionally.

Stir in the pasta, beans, and green beans, and simmer for 10 to 15 minutes more until the pasta is al dente. Occasionally stir the soup while it cooks.

Let the soup sit for 10 minutes before serving. Serve with warm Italian bread. Pass the Parmesan cheese at the table.

Yield: 8 servings

Soup Tips

If fresh herbs are available, add 2 or 3 tablespoons of chopped fresh basil or arugula at the finish. Fresh greens, such as escarole or kale, can also be added 10 minutes before the end (about 2 cups cut chiffonade or chopped). Ditalini and tubettini are miniature pastas available in the pasta section of most grocery stores.

Greek Village Bean Soup (Fassoulada)

There are myriad versions of this Greek village soup, but all contain small white beans and hearty vegetables. (Fassoul refers to beans.) It is a soup for the seasons, so if other vegetables such as carrots, celery, or turnips are available, by all means use them.

1	cup dried navy beans or other small white beans, soaked overnight and drained
8	to 10 cups water
1	tablespoon canola oil
1	medium yellow onion, chopped
1	red bell pepper, seeded and diced
2	or 3 cloves garlic, minced
1	medium white potato, diced (peeled if desired)
1/4	cup tomato paste
1 1/2	tablespoons dried parsley
1	teaspoon ground cumin
1	teaspoon dried thyme
1/2	teaspoon ground black pepper
1/2	teaspoon salt
2	cups coarsely chopped Swiss chard or spinach
1/4	pound feta cheese, crumbled (optional)

Combine the beans and water in a large saucepan and bring to a simmer. Cook for 1 to 1½ hours over low heat, until the beans are tender. Drain, reserving 6 cups of the cooking liquid. (Add more water if necessary.)

In a large saucepan heat the oil. Add the onion, bell pepper, and garlic, and sauté for 5 minutes. Add the beans, cooking liquid, potato, tomato paste, and seasonings, and bring to a simmer. Cook for 20 to 25 minutes over medium-low heat, stirring occasionally. Stir in the Swiss chard and cook for about 10 minutes more.

Let the soup sit for 10 minutes before ladling into bowls. If desired, sprinkle feta cheese over the top.

Yield: 8 servings

Sunday Supper Soup

On a lazy Sunday afternoon, making soup can be a form of therapy. Simply load up the pot with vegetables left over from the weekend, add various pantry sundries such as beans and rice, zealously spice it up, and simmer the whole thing together. You'll clear out your refrigerator and prepare a satisfying, low-stress meal at the same time.

1	tablespoon canola oil
1	medium yellow onion, diced
6	or 8 mushrooms, sliced
1/2	medium zucchini or yellow squash, coarsely chopped
2	cloves garlic, minced
1	jalapeño or serrano chile, seeded and minced (optional)
6	cups water
1	medium carrot, peeled and diced
1	medium white or sweet potato, diced
1/4	cup white rice or miniature pasta (tubettini or orzo)
1	tablespoon dried parsley
1 1/2	teaspoons dried oregano
1/2	teaspoon ground black pepper
1/2	teaspoon salt
1	(15-ounce) can chickpeas or red or white kidney beans, drained
2	cups coarsely chopped leafy greens (spinach, kale, collards, or escarole)

In a large saucepan heat the oil. Add the onion, mushrooms, zucchini, garlic, and chile, and sauté for 5 to 7 minutes. Add the water, carrot, potato, rice or pasta, and seasonings, and bring to a simmer. (If using collard greens, add them now.) Cook for 20 to 25 minutes over medium-low heat, stirring occasionally.

Stir in the beans and greens and cook for 10 minutes more, stirring occasionally. Let the soup sit for 10 minutes before serving. Serve with warm bread and a tossed salad.

Yield: 6 servings

Soup Tips

This version is just one of many potential supper soups available to the resourceful cook. Feel free to add celery or bell peppers, replace the potato with winter squash, use quinoa for the rice, or thicken the soup with leftover tomato paste or sauce. Leave some of the mushrooms whole for a wholesome and laid-back appearance.

Mondo Chili

A steaming salubrious bowl of chili takes the bite out of a harsh winter day and restores a sense of optimism to one's personal world order. I like to spice up chili with unfettered exuberance, and I always alert people around me that I will be back for second helpings.

1   tablespoon canola oil
1   large yellow onion, diced
1   green bell pepper, seeded and diced
1   red bell pepper, seeded and diced
1   cup sliced celery
2   cloves garlic, minced
1   (28-ounce) can crushed tomatoes
1   (15-ounce) can red kidney beans, drained
1   (14-ounce) can stewed tomatoes, diced
1   to 1 1/2 tablespoons chili powder
1   tablespoon dried oregano
2 1/2 teaspoons ground cumin
1   teaspoon paprika
1   teaspoon salt
1   to 2 teaspoons Tabasco or other bottled hot sauce
1/2   teaspoon ground black pepper

In a large saucepan heat the oil. Add the onion, bell peppers, celery, and garlic, and sauté for 6 to 8 minutes, until the vegetables are tender. Stir in the crushed tomatoes, beans, stewed tomatoes, and seasonings, and simmer for 25 to 30 minutes over low heat, stirring occasionally. Set aside for 5 to 10 minutes before serving.

Ladle the chili into bowls and serve with Quintessential Corn Bread (page 239).

Yield: 4 to 6 servings

Soup Tips

You can serve a variety of toppings with this chili, such as shredded lowfat cheddar or Monterey Jack cheese, chopped scallions, red onion, or salsa.

Tomato Lentil Zuppa with Orzo

When my mother says zuppa (an Italian word for soup), she is talking about this rustic cauldron. Lentils, orzo (tiny football-shaped pasta), tomatoes, and herbs meld in a harmonious and filling combination.

1/2 cup lentils
6 cups water
1 tablespoon olive oil
1 medium yellow onion, diced
1 celery stalk, chopped
2 or 3 cloves garlic, minced
2 cups diced white potatoes
1 (14-ounce) can stewed tomatoes (or 2 large tomatoes, diced)
5 to 6 tablespoons canned tomato paste
1 tablespoon dried oregano
2 teaspoons dried basil
1 teaspoon salt
1/2 teaspoon ground black pepper
1/4 cup orzo pasta (*rosa marina*)
1/4 pound green beans, trimmed and cut into 1-inch pieces

In a medium saucepan combine the lentils and water and bring to a simmer. Cook for 40 to 45 minutes over medium-low heat, stirring occasionally, until the lentils are tender. Drain, reserving 4 cups of the cooking liquid. (If less than 4 cups, add hot water.)

In a large saucepan heat the oil. Add the onion, celery, and garlic, and sauté for 5 minutes. Add the lentils, cooking liquid, potatoes, stewed tomatoes, tomato paste, and seasonings, and bring to a simmer. Cook for 20 to 25 minutes over medium-low heat, stirring occasionally.

Stir in the pasta and green beans, and simmer for 10 to 15 minutes more until the pasta is al dente. Occasionally stir the soup while it cooks.

Let the soup sit for 10 minutes before serving. Serve with warm Italian bread.

Yield: 6 to 8 servings

Soup Tips

You can also add chopped spinach or kale to the soup 10 minutes before the finish. Grated Parmesan or Romano cheese can be offered as a topping.

Indonesian Peanut Soup

Coconut and peanut butter collude to form a doubly rich, nutty soup. Ketjap manis, a sweetened soy sauce, provides a distinctive Indonesian flavor. An aromatic rice makes a compatible partner for the soup.

1	tablespoon canola oil
1	medium yellow onion, diced
2	cloves garlic, minced
1	to 2 chile peppers, seeded and minced
2	teaspoons minced fresh ginger
2	teaspoons minced fresh lemon grass
4	cups water
1 1/2	cups lowfat coconut milk
1/3	cup chunky peanut butter
1/4	cup *ketjap manis* or soy sauce
2	tablespoons lime juice
1	teaspoon ground coriander
1	teaspoon ground cumin
1/2	teaspoon ground black pepper
2	tablespoons chopped cilantro

In a large saucepan heat the oil. Add the onion, garlic, chile pepper, ginger, and lemon grass, and sauté for 4 minutes. Add the water and bring to a simmer. Cook for 12 to 15 minutes over medium-low heat, stirring occasionally. Reduce the heat, add the coconut milk, peanut butter, *ketjap manis*, lime juice, and dried seasonings, and cook for 5 to 10 minutes more over low heat, stirring frequently. Stir in the cilantro.

Ladle into bowls and serve hot with jasmine or basmati rice.

Yield: 6 to 8 servings

Soup Tips

Look for *ketjap manis* and lemon grass in well-stocked Asian grocery stores.

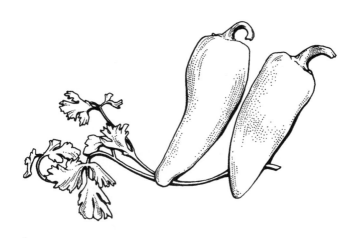

Hoppin' John Soup

This wintry soup was inspired (of course) by the Southern dish of black-eyed peas and rice.

1	tablespoon canola oil
1	medium yellow onion, diced
1	large stalk celery, chopped
2	or 3 cloves garlic, minced
6	cups water
2	medium carrots, peeled and diced
1	medium parsnip, peeled and diced
1	medium sweet potato, diced
1 1/2	tablespoons dried parsley
2	teaspoons dried oregano
1/2	teaspoon salt
1/2	teaspoon ground black pepper
1/3	cup long grain white rice
1	(15-ounce) can black-eyed peas, drained

In a large saucepan heat the oil. Add the onion, celery, and garlic, and sauté for 5 minutes. Add the water, carrots, parsnip, potato, and seasonings, and bring to a simmer. Cook for 10 minutes over medium-low heat, stirring occasionally. Stir in the rice and cook for 20 minutes more, stirring occasionally, until the rice and vegetables are tender. Stir in the black-eyed peas and cook for 5 minutes more over low heat. Remove from the heat and let stand for 10 minutes.

Ladle into bowls and serve with warm bread.

Yield: 6 servings

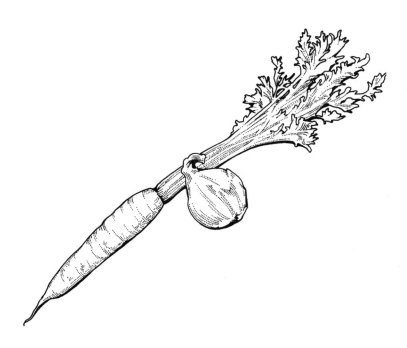

Sizzling Black Bean Soup

For as long as I have a been a chef, I have loved black bean soups. These legumes have an earthy flavor and meld easily into a wide variety of broths and stews. Black bean soups are also amenable to a range of spices, herbs, and chile peppers. This Southwestern-inspired soup is radiant with exhilarating flavors.

1 1/2 cups dried black beans, soaked overnight and drained
6   cups water
1   tablespoon canola oil
1   large yellow onion, diced
1   green or red bell pepper, seeded and diced
1   large stalk celery, chopped
3   to 4 cloves garlic, minced
1   jalapeño pepper, seeded and minced
2   medium carrots, peeled and diced
2   to 3 tablespoons minced fresh parsley
1   tablespoon dried oregano
1 1/2 teaspoons ground cumin
1   teaspoon ground coriander
1   teaspoon dried thyme
1/2 teaspoon ground black pepper
1/2 cup canned crushed tomatoes
1   teaspoon salt
2   tablespoons chopped fresh cilantro

In a medium saucepan combine the beans and water, and bring to a simmer. Cook for 1 to 1½ hours over medium-low heat until the beans are tender. Drain the beans, reserving 4 cups of the cooking liquid.

In a large saucepan heat the oil. Add the onion, bell pepper, celery, garlic, and jalapeño, and sauté for 5 minutes. Add the beans, cooking liquid, carrots, and seasonings (except the salt and cilantro). Bring to a simmer and cook for about 20 minutes over low heat, stirring occasionally.

Stir in the crushed tomatoes, salt, and cilantro, and cook for 10 minutes more, stirring occasionally. Remove from the heat and let stand for 10 minutes. (If you prefer a thick soup, puree half of the soup in a blender or food processor fitted with a steel blade and return to the pan.)

Ladle the soup into bowls. If you'd like, serve with warm flour tortillas and lowfat plain yogurt.

Yield: 6 servings

Soup Tips

Soak the beans in plenty of water before cooking. Soaking yields fuller, plumper beans and reduces the cooking time. After draining, cook the beans in fresh water.

West African Groundnut Stew

This classic soup displays the versatility of groundnuts (otherwise known as peanuts). In West African kitchens groundnuts are pureed into pastes and added to soups, sauces, and stews. This aromatic version is fortified with ginger, tomatoes, and sweet potato. Couscous, a fluffy North African seminola grainlike pasta, makes a natural accompaniment.

1	tablespoon canola oil
1	medium yellow onion, diced
1	yellow or red bell pepper, seeded and diced
2	cloves garlic, minced
2	teaspoons minced fresh ginger
1	cayenne or serrano chile, seeded and minced
2	cups water
2	cups tomato juice
1	(14-ounce) can stewed tomatoes
1	medium sweet potato, diced (about 2 cups)
1	tablespoon dried parsley
1 1/2	teaspoons dried thyme
1 1/2	teaspoons ground cumin
1/2	teaspoon salt
1/2	cup chunky peanut butter (preferably unsweetened)
2	cups shredded red Swiss chard or spinach

In a large saucepan heat the oil. Add the onion, bell pepper, garlic, ginger, and chile, and sauté for 4 to 5 minutes. Stir in the water, tomato juice, stewed tomatoes, sweet potato, and seasonings, and cook for 25 minutes over medium-low heat, stirring occasionally, until the potato is tender.

Aggressively stir in the peanut butter. Stir in the chard and return to a gentle simmer, stirring frequently. Remove the stew from the heat and let stand for 5 to 10 minutes.

Ladle into bowls and serve with a bowl of couscous or rice and roasted plantains.

Yield: 6 servings

Soup Tips

For last-minute garnish, top each bowl of soup with a tablespoon of roasted, chopped peanuts and scallions.

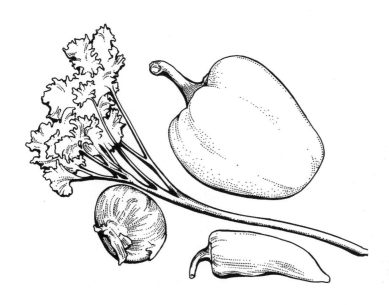

Fava Bean Ribollita

Ribollita, a well-cooked soup ladled over bread, is similar to Heartry Vegetable Panade (page 192). This ribollita, which means "reboiled" in Italian, features large fava beans, a mealy, earthy legume prevalent in European kitchens. There are no firm rules for ribollita, however; whatever's in season or in the pantry is fair game.

1   tablespoon olive oil
1   medium yellow onion, diced
2   or 3 cloves garlic, minced
1   small zucchini, diced
1   cup shredded red or white cabbage
2   medium carrots, peeled and diced
6   cups water
1   (28-ounce) can whole tomatoes
2   cups diced white potatoes (do not peel)
2   teaspoons dried basil
2   teaspoons dried oregano
1   teaspoon ground sage
1/2   teaspoon salt
1/2   teaspoon ground black pepper
1   (15-ounce) can large fava beans or Roman beans, drained
1/4   pound fresh green beans, trimmed and cut into 1-inch pieces
1   small firm loaf of Italian bread, torn into pieces
1/2   cup grated Parmesan cheese (optional)

In a large saucepan heat the oil. Add the onion and garlic, and sauté for 4 minutes. Add the zucchini, cabbage, and carrots, and cook over medium heat for about 10 minutes, stirring frequently. Stir in the water, canned tomatoes, potatoes, and seasonings, and bring to a simmer. Cook for about 45 minutes over medium-low heat, stirring occasionally. Stir in the fava beans and green beans, and simmer for 10 minutes more.

Remove from the heat and let stand for several minutes. Serve now or cover and chill for later reheating.

To serve, place the torn bread into the bottom of each soup bowl. Ladle the soup over the bread and pack it down with a spoon. Let the soup sit for a few minutes, allowing the bread to soak in the broth. If desired, pass the cheese at the table.

Yield: 8 servings

Thai Black Rice Soup

*This tureen features black rice, an aromatic grain popular in
Southeast Asian cuisine. It produces a chocolate-colored
broth, warmly accented with hints of lemon grass, coconut,
chiles, and penetrating herbs and spices. These sultry flavors
tantalize the taste buds with ripples of pleasure.*

1	tablespoon canola oil or peanut oil
1	small yellow onion, finely chopped
1	medium red bell pepper, seeded and chopped
12	button mushrooms, sliced
2	cloves garlic, minced
2	teaspoons minced fresh lemon grass
1	Thai chile or other chile pepper, seeded and minced (optional)
4	cups water
2	medium carrots, peeled and diced
1/3	cup black rice or black rice blend
3	to 4 tablespoons light soy sauce
1	teaspoon ground cumin
1	teaspoon ground coriander
1	cup lowfat coconut milk
2	tablespoons chopped cilantro
2	tablespoons chopped fresh Thai basil or opal basil (optional)
	Juice of 1 lime

In a large saucepan heat the oil. Add the onion, bell pepper, mushrooms, garlic, lemon grass, and chile, and sauté for 5 to 7 minutes. Stir in the water, carrots, rice, soy sauce, and seasonings, and cook for 45 to 50 minutes over medium-low heat, stirring occasionally.

Stir in the coconut milk, cilantro, basil, and lime juice, and return to a gentle simmer. Remove from the heat and set aside for 5 to 10 minutes.

Ladle the soup into bowls and serve hot.

Yield: 6 servings

Soup Tips

This is a brothy soup; if you prefer a thicker soup, combine 1 teaspoon of cornstarch with 1 teaspoon warm water and whisk into the broth with the coconut milk. Black rice is available in well-stocked Asian markets, natural food stores, and gourmet groceries.

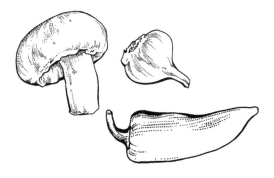

Smoky Brazilian Black Bean Soup

¡Viva Brazil! You can enjoy this soup any time of the year, but it is an especially proper remedy for chilly days. Chipotle chiles are used in place of the traditional dried meats usually found in Brazilian bean soups; the chiles add a smoky, spicy flavor and are far more interesting than meat.

1	cup dried black beans, soaked overnight and drained
8	cups water
1	tablespoon canola oil
1	medium yellow onion, diced
1	red or green bell pepper, seeded and diced
2	or 3 cloves garlic, minced
1	large tomato, diced
1	canned chipotle pepper, seeded and chopped
2	medium carrots, peeled and diced
1/4	cup tomato paste
2	teaspoons ground cumin
2	teaspoons dried oregano
1	teaspoon dried thyme
1	teaspoon salt
1/4	cup chopped fresh parsley

In a large saucepan combine the beans and water, and bring to a simmer. Cook for 1 to 1 1/2 hours over medium-low heat until tender. Drain, reserving 4 cups of the cooking liquid.

In another large saucepan heat the oil. Add the onion, bell pepper, and garlic, and sauté for 5 minutes. Stir in the tomato and chipotle pepper, and sauté for 2 minutes more. Stir in the beans, cooking liquid, carrots, tomato paste, cumin, oregano, and thyme, and cook for 25 to 30 minutes over medium-low heat, stirring occasionally. Stir in the salt and parsley and cook for 5 to 10 minutes more. Remove from the heat and let stand for 10 minutes before serving. Mash some of the beans against the side of the pan to thicken the broth.

Ladle into bowls and serve with warm bread. Rice makes a fitting accompaniment.

Yield: 6 servings

Chunky Red and Black Bean Chili with Seitan

Seitan gives this meatless "bowl of red" a meatlike chewiness and texture. Seitan is a protein-rich gluten product with the starch removed. Its high protein content makes seitan a popular meat analog.

1	tablespoon canola oil
1	medium yellow onion, diced
1	green bell pepper, seeded and diced
2	celery stalks, chopped
2	cloves garlic, minced
1	(28-ounce) can crushed tomatoes
1	(15-ounce) can black beans, drained
1	(15-ounce) can red kidney beans, drained
1/2	cup water
1/4	pound *seitan,* diced
1	tablespoon chili powder
1	tablespoon dried parsley
1	tablespoon dried oregano
2	teaspoons ground cumin
1/2	teaspoon ground black pepper
1/2	teaspoon salt
1	cup shredded lowfat Monterey Jack or provolone cheese

In a large saucepan heat the oil. Add the onion, bell pepper, celery, and garlic, and sauté for 5 to 7 minutes. Stir in the crushed tomatoes, beans, water, *seitan,* and seasonings, and cook for about 25 minutes over low heat, stirring occasionally. Let the chili stand for 10 minutes before serving.

Ladle the chili into bowls and top with the shredded cheese.

Yield: 6 servings

Soup Tips

Look for *seitan* in the refrigerated section of well-stocked natural food stores and supermarkets.

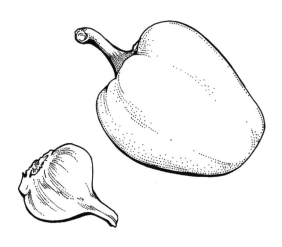

Chapter 5

Savory Soups in the Springtime

Spring symbolizes rebirth, renewal, and optimism. It is the season for budding tulips and blossoming trees, warm afternoons and friendly breezes. Fresh vegetables, greens, and herbs reappear at the marketplace and sprout up in once dormant gardens. As the spirit of winter bids adieu, spring ushers in a lighter, kinder, more enlightened fare.

Springtime soups and stews tap into the sundries of the season: asparagus, arugula, wild mushrooms, early leafy greens, and broccoli are prevalent. When teamed up with perennial favorites—legumes, pastas, potatoes, and root vegetables—a plethora of soup meals ensues. Spring soups are a touch lighter but just as satisfying.

This chapter is filled with versatile and appealing bowls ideal for both April showers and May flowers. There is earthy and rustic Wild Mushroom and Barley Soup, Minestrone with Arugula Pesto, and Curried Potato and Green Pea Soup. For sophisticated tastes, Artichoke and White Bean Stew and Emily's Asparagus Vichyssoise, and others aptly fill the bill. Spanish *Caldo Gallego* and Mexican *Sopa de Fideo* add a taste of global cuisine.

Whether the forecast calls for baseball caps or earmuffs, sweaters or winter overcoats, there are plenty of springtime soups, stews, and bisques offered here to whet your expectant palate. When spring is in the air and soup is on the stove, life can be very good, indeed.

Wild Mushroom and Barley Soup

Mushrooms are in vogue: there has been an avalanche of fancy wild mushrooms at the green grocer's. This is a boon for soup epicures; mushrooms add woodsy, earthy flavors and sturdy textures to a variety of soup meals, including this hearty barley tureen.

1	tablespoon canola oil
12	ounces button mushrooms, sliced
4	ounces fresh shiitake or oyster mushrooms, sliced
4	ounces Italian brown mushrooms (cremini), sliced
1	medium yellow onion, diced
2	stalks celery, chopped
2	tablespoons chopped shallots
6	cups hot water
1/2	cup pearl barley
1/4	cup dry white wine
2	teaspoons Dijon-style mustard
2	tablespoons dried parsley
1	teaspoon dried thyme
1/2	teaspoon salt
1/2	teaspoon ground white pepper or black pepper
1/3	pound green beans, trimmed and cut into 1-inch pieces

In a large saucepan heat the oil. Add the mushrooms, onion, celery, and shallots, and cook for 8 to 10 minutes over medium heat, stirring frequently. Add the water, barley, wine, mustard, and seasonings, and cook for about 50 minutes over low heat, stirring occasionally. Stir in the green beans and cook for 10 minutes more.

Let the soup stand for several minutes before serving. Ladle into bowls and serve with dark bread.

Yield: 6 servings

Soup Tips
Fresh shiitake, oyster, and Italian brown mushrooms can be found at well-stocked supermarkets and natural food stores.

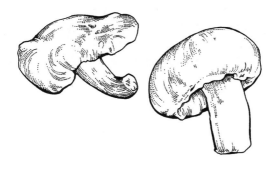

Lean Green Vichyssoise

This forest green soup radiates with the grassy aroma and nutritious flavors of leafy vegetables. I like to add an assertive herb such as arugula or dill for a last-minute infusion of flavor. The luscious texture of this vichyssoise is accomplished without a drop of fat-laden cream or butter.

1	tablespoon canola oil
1	medium yellow onion, diced
2	cups rinsed and chopped leeks
1	large stalk celery, sliced
2	cloves garlic, minced
6	cups water
4	cups peeled and diced white potatoes
1/4	cup dry white wine
1 1/2	tablespoons dried parsley
1	teaspoon dried thyme
3/4	teaspoon salt
1/2	teaspoon ground black pepper
2	cups coarsely chopped spinach leaves (trimmed)
2	cups coarsely chopped kale
1/4	cup chopped arugula or 2 tablespoons chopped dill

In a large saucepan heat the oil. Add the onion, leeks, celery, and garlic, and sauté for 5 to 7 minutes. Add the water, potatoes, wine, and seasonings, and cook for 20 to 25 minutes over low heat, stirring occasionally, until the potatoes are tender. Stir in the spinach, kale, and fresh herbs, and cook for 5 to 10 minutes more.

Transfer the soup to a blender or food processor fitted with a steel blade and puree until smooth. Return to the pan and keep hot until ready to serve, or chill for later and serve as a cold soup.

Yield: 6 to 8 servings

Soupe au Pistou

When reading a good book, most people like to cuddle up on a big couch. I like to sip from a big bowl of soup. While immersed in A Year in Provence by Peter Mayle, I was inspired to make this Provençal vegetable soup. Pistou is an intensely flavored paste of basil, garlic, and cheese; it is swirled into the soup at the last minute. The soup (and the book) brought warmth and comfort.

For the soup:
1   tablespoon canola oil
1   medium yellow onion, diced
2   stalks celery, sliced
2   cups rinsed and chopped leeks
6   cups water
2   cups diced white potatoes (peeled if desired)
2   tablespoons dried parsley
2   teaspoons dried basil
1   teaspoon salt
1/2 teaspoon ground white pepper
1/4 pound green string beans, trimmed and cut into 1-inch sections
1   (15-ounce) can cannellini beans or other white beans, drained
1/2 cup miniature pasta spirals, tubettini or soup shells

For the pistou:
6   to 8 cloves garlic, minced
1 1/2 cups packed basil leaves, coarsely chopped (chiffonade style)
1/3 cup olive oil
1/3 to 1/2 cup grated Parmesan cheese

In a large saucepan heat the oil. Add the onion, celery, and leeks, and sauté for about 7 minutes. Add the water, potatoes, and seasonings, and bring to a simmer. Cook for 20 to 25 minutes over medium-low heat, stirring occasionally. Add the green beans, white beans, and pasta, and cook for about 15 minutes more over low heat, stirring occasionally.

Meanwhile, make the *pistou*. Crush the garlic and basil together in a food mill, bowl, or blender. Blend in the oil and cheese, forming a paste. Transfer to a serving bowl.

To serve, ladle the soup into bowls and swirl a small spoonful of *pistou* into each. Serve with French bread.

Yield: 6 to 8 servings

Soup Tips

The ingredients for *soupe au pistou* vary by the season; feel free to add diced parsnips, carrots, zucchini, butternut squash, or whatever is available.

Minestrone with Arugula Pesto

Minestrone is a classic Italian soup meal that can be prepared in myriad ways. This hearty version is brightened up with a garlicky pesto infused with arugula, a peppery leaf. The pesto is swirled into the soup at the last minute.

For the soup:
1 tablespoon olive oil
1 medium yellow onion, diced
2 cups diced eggplant or zucchini
8 to 12 mushrooms, sliced
6 cups hot water
1 (14-ounce) can stewed tomatoes
1 large white potato, diced (peeled if desired)
1/4 cup tomato paste
2 teaspoons dried oregano
2 teaspoons dried basil
3/4 teaspoon salt
1/2 teaspoon ground black pepper
1/2 cup tubettini or orzo pasta

For the pesto:
4 to 6 cloves garlic, minced
1 1/2 cups packed arugula, coarsely chopped
1/3 cup finely chopped almonds or walnuts
1/3 to 1/2 cup olive oil
1/4 to 1/2 cup grated Parmesan cheese

In a large saucepan heat the oil. Add the onion, eggplant, and mushrooms, and cook over medium heat for 8 to 10 minutes, stirring frequently. Stir in the water, stewed tomatoes, potato, tomato paste, and seasonings, and bring to a simmer. Cook for about 20 minutes over medium-low heat, stirring occasionally. Stir in the pasta and cook for 10 to 12 minutes more, stirring frequently. Set aside for 10 minutes before serving.

Meanwhile, make the pesto. Puree the garlic, arugula, and nuts together in a bowl, food processor fitted with a steel blade, or blender. Blend in the oil and cheese, forming a paste. Transfer to a serving bowl.

Ladle the minestrone into bowls and swirl a small spoonful of pesto into each bowl. Serve with warm Italian bread.

Yield: 6 to 8 servings

Soup Tips

I also like to add a 15-ounce can of cannellini beans (drained) near the finish. Arugula, also called rocket or roquette, can be found in the specialty produce sections of well-stocked supermarkets. If arugula is unavailable, try a combination of basil and watercress.

Spring Vegetable and Matzo Ball Soup

Matzo ball soup is the signature soup of Jewish kitchens. The reputation of some Jewish delis hinges upon their matzo ball soup. Although traditionally prepared with chicken broth, this healthful variation showcases the flavors of spring vegetables. Matzo balls—dumplings made with matzo meal, an unleavened flour—provide major sustenance.

1	tablespoon canola oil
1	medium yellow onion, chopped
2	cups rinsed and chopped leeks
2	stalks celery, chopped
1	red bell pepper, seeded and diced
2	or 3 cloves garlic, minced
8	cups water or vegetable stock
4	medium carrots, peeled and diced
1	teaspoon salt
1/2	teaspoon ground black pepper
6	to 8 asparagus spears, trimmed and cut into 1-inch pieces
1/4	cup chopped fresh parsley
8	to 12 cooked matzo balls (see recipe)

In a large saucepan heat the oil. Add the onion, leeks, celery, bell pepper, and garlic, and sauté for 5 to 7 minutes. Stir in the water, carrots, and dried seasonings, and bring to a simmer. Cook over medium-low heat for 20 minutes, stirring occasionally.

Add the asparagus and parsley, and cook for 5 to 10 minutes more over low heat. Remove from the heat and set aside until the matzo balls are ready. (The soup can be made a day ahead of time and refrigerated.)

Vegetarian Soup Cuisine

Return the soup to a simmer and gently add the cooked matzo balls; cook for 10 to 15 minutes more over low heat. To serve, place a matzo ball in each bowl and ladle the soup over the top.

Yield: 8 servings

Matzo Balls

3	large eggs
3	tablespoons canola oil
3/4	cup matzo meal
1	teaspoon salt (optional)
3	tablespoons water

In a medium mixing bowl beat the eggs. Add the oil and beat again. Fold in the matzo meal and salt (if desired). Blend in the water. Cover the dough and refrigerate for about 15 minutes.

In a large saucepan bring about 2 quarts of water to a boil. Remove the matzo dough from the refrigerator. Using moistened hands, form the dough into small balls and drop into the boiling water. Cover the pan and cook over medium-low heat for about 30 minutes. Drain the liquid and let the balls cool to room temperature. Refrigerate until ready to serve with the soup.

Watercress and Potato Chowder

Watercress is a delicate spring green with a faint peppery presence. Although watercress is more commonly used as a salad garnish, the leaves also bring a light herbal touch to soups and chowders. In this offering, a dash of vinegar perks up the soup near the finish.

2	medium bunches watercress
1	tablespoon canola oil
1	medium yellow onion, chopped
2	stalks celery, chopped
2	cloves garlic, minced
4	cups hot water
4	cups diced white potatoes (peeled, if desired)
2	medium carrots, peeled and diced
1 1/2	teaspoons dried thyme
1/2	teaspoon ground white pepper or black pepper
1	teaspoon salt
1	cup whole or lowfat milk
1/4	cup chopped fresh parsley
1	to 2 tablespoons rice vinegar or balsamic vinegar

Place the watercress in a colander and rinse under cold running water; drain and pat dry. Remove the woody stems and coarsely chop the leaves. Set aside.

In a large saucepan heat the oil. Add the onion, celery, and garlic, and sauté for 5 to 7 minutes. Stir in the water, potatoes, carrots, and dried seasonings, and bring to a simmer. Cook for 20 minutes over low-medium heat, stirring occasionally.

Stir in the watercress, milk, and parsley, and cook for 5 to 10 minutes more over low heat, stirring frequently. (Do not boil.) To thicken the soup, mash the potatoes against the side of the pan with a wooden spoon. Stir in the vinegar. Turn off the heat and let sit for about 10 minutes before serving.

Ladle the soup into bowls and serve hot.

Yield: 6 servings

Soup Tips
A sprinkling of grated Parmesan cheese makes a nice last-minute topping.

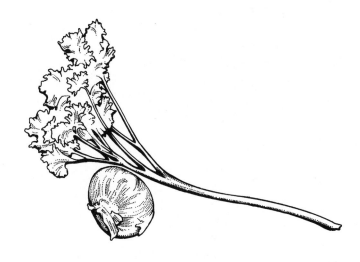

Whole Grain Rice and Mushroom Soup

Whole grain rices are excellent sources of complex carbo-hydrates, dietary fiber, and other nutrients. They also supply high-octane, long-lasting energy. Their longer cooking times are compatible with well-cooked soups like this mushroom tureen.

1	tablespoon canola oil
12	ounces button mushrooms, sliced
4	ounces fresh oyster mushrooms or shiitake mush-rooms, sliced
1	medium yellow onion, diced
1	large red bell pepper, seeded and diced
2	cloves garlic, minced
6	cups hot water
1/2	cup brown rice, Wehani, or black rice blend
1/4	cup dry white wine or sherry
1	teaspoon Dijon-style mustard
1	tablespoon dried parsley (or 2 tablespoons chopped fresh parsley)
1	teaspoon dried thyme
1	teaspoon salt
1/2	teaspoon ground black pepper
2	cups chopped kale or spinach

In a large saucepan heat the oil. Add the mushrooms, onion, bell pepper, and garlic, and cook for 8 to 10 minutes over medium heat, stirring frequently. Add the water, rice, wine, mustard, and seasonings, and cook for 50 minutes to 1 hour over low heat, stirring occasionally.

Stir in the kale and cook for 5 to 10 minutes more. Let the soup stand for several minutes before serving.

Ladle into bowls and serve with dark bread.

Yield: 6 servings

Soup Tips
Fresh shiitake or oyster mushrooms can be found at well-stocked supermarkets and natural food stores.

Sopa de Fideo
(Mexican Noodle Soup)

Upon learning that I was making sopa de fideo, my friend Jessica Robin made a face that was not entirely consistent with avid anticipation. It seems she subsisted on this sopa during her Peace Corps days in Bolivia. The soup she remembered was mostly noodles in bland liquid. This piquant version, laden with vegetables and aromatic spices, regained her confidence.

1	tablespoon canola oil
1	medium yellow onion, diced
1	large red or green bell pepper, seeded and diced
2	stalks celery, chopped
2	or 3 cloves garlic, minced
1	jalapeño or serrano chile, seeded and minced
8	cups water or vegetable stock
1	large white potato, diced
2	medium carrots, peeled and diced
1	(14-ounce) can stewed tomatoes
2	tablespoons dried parsley (or 4 tablespoons chopped fresh parsley)
1	tablespoon dried oregano
2	teaspoons ground cumin
1	teaspoon salt
1/2	teaspoon ground black pepper
4	ounces angel-hair pasta
1/2	cup shredded Monterey Jack or Colby cheese
8	(6-inch) flour tortillas, warmed

In a large saucepan heat the oil. Add the onion, bell pepper, celery, garlic, and chile pepper, and cook for 8 to 10 minutes over medium heat, stirring frequently. Add the water, potato, carrots, stewed tomatoes, and dried seasonings, and bring to a simmer. Cook for 30 to 35 minutes over medium-low heat, stirring occasionally.

Snap the pasta in half and stir into the soup. Cook for 10 to 12 minutes over medium heat until the pasta is al dente. Let the soup stand for a few minutes before serving. (If using fresh parsley, add it now.)

Ladle into bowls and top with shredded cheese. Serve with warm flour tortillas.

Yield: 6 to 8 servings

Soup Tips

A few tablespoons of chopped fresh cilantro or a Mexican herb called epazote may also be added near the finish.

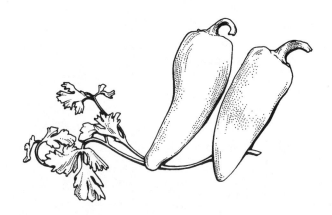

Miso and Asian Greens Soup

Miso is a fermented soybean paste used to flavor Japanese soups. It is high in protein, low in fat, and has an extremely long shelf life. Japanese soups also call for kombu, a dried, edible seaweed. Like sun-dried tomatoes or dried chiles, kombu must be soaked in water before being added to soups.

1	tablespoon canola oil or peanut oil
1	medium onion, finely chopped
2	large carrots, peeled and sliced thinly at an angle
2	cloves garlic, minced
1	teaspoon minced fresh ginger
6	cups water, vegetable stock, or dashi
2	(8-inch) strips kombu, soaked in warm water for 1 hour
4	to 6 scallions, chopped
1	(2-inch) section of daikon, peeled and sliced thin
2	cups coarsely chopped bok choy, pat soi, or red shen choy
2	cups shredded Chinese cabbage
1/2	teaspoon ground black pepper
2	to 3 tablespoons miso paste

In a large saucepan heat the oil. Add the onion, carrots, garlic, and ginger, and sauté for 5 minutes. Add the water, kombu, half of the scallions, and the daikon, and bring to a simmer. Cook over medium heat for about 15 minutes, stirring occasionally. Stir in the greens and ground pepper, and cook for 12 to 15 minutes more over medium-low heat, stirring occasionally.

Meanwhile, dissolve the miso paste in 2 to 3 tablespoons warm water. At the last minute, remove the kombu and stir the miso paste into the soup. Do not boil the soup once the miso paste has been added.

Ladle the soup into large soup bowls and top with the remaining scallions.

Yield: 6 servings

Soup Tips

Miso can be found in Asian markets and in the soy sauce section of well-stocked grocery stores. Dashi is a stock made by simmering water and kombu together for 20 to 30 minutes. The resulting liquid forms the base of most Japanese soups and sauces.

Mexican Tortilla and Corn Soup

Called sopa de tortilla, this classic Mexican soup is a spicy broth of vegetables, chiles, corn, and strips of flour tortillas. When simmered in liquid, tortillas bear a marked resemblance to noodles. A touch of Monterey Jack cheese nicely complements the piquant broth, and cilantro tickles the palate at the finish.

1	tablespoon canola oil
1	medium yellow onion, diced
1	small zucchini, diced
1	red bell pepper, seeded and diced
2	cloves garlic, minced
1	to 2 jalapeño or serrano chiles, seeded and minced
6	cups water or vegetable stock
1	(14-ounce) can stewed tomatoes
2	teaspoons dried oregano
1 1/2	teaspoons ground cumin
3/4	teaspoon salt
1 1/2	cups corn kernels, fresh or frozen
4	(6-inch) flour tortillas, halved and cut into 1/2-inch-wide strips
2	tablespoons chopped fresh cilantro
1/2	to 1 cup shredded lowfat Monterey Jack cheese (optional)

In a large saucepan heat the oil. Add the onion, zucchini, bell pepper, garlic, and chiles, and sauté for 5 to 7 minutes. Add the water, stewed tomatoes, and seasonings, and bring to a simmer. Reduce the heat to low and cook for 15 minutes, stirring occasionally. Stir in the corn and flour tortillas, and cook for 10 to 15 minutes more. Stir in the cilantro and let stand for 5 minutes before serving.

Ladle into bowls; if desired, sprinkle the cheese over the top.

Yield: 6 servings

Soup Tips

For a slight variation, add a roasted poblano (or ancho) chile in place of the jalapeño. If you happen to locate epazote, a hard-to-find Mexican herb, by all means add 1 or 2 tablespoons (chopped) to the soup with the cilantro.

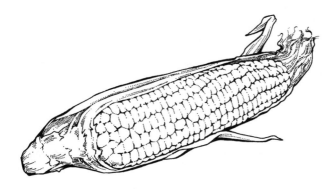

Romaine and Potato Chowder

*I am an unabashed lover of crisp leafy greens and do not limit
their appearances to tossed salads. This hearty soup offers
vivid proof that salad greens and soup go hand in hand.*

1	tablespoon olive oil
1	medium yellow onion, chopped
1	red bell pepper, seeded and diced
2	stalks celery, chopped
2	medium carrots, peeled and diced
3	or 4 cloves garlic, minced
6	cups water
4	cups diced white potatoes (peeled if desired)
1 1/2	teaspoons dried thyme
1/2	teaspoon ground white pepper or black pepper
1/2	teaspoon salt
1	small bunch Romaine lettuce or escarole, rinsed and shredded (chiffonade style)
1/4	cup chopped fresh parsley
1	to 2 tablespoons red wine vinegar (optional)

In a large saucepan heat the oil. Add the onion, bell pepper, celery, carrots, and garlic, and sauté for 5 to 7 minutes. Stir in the water, potatoes, and dried seasonings, and bring to a simmer. Cook for 20 to 25 minutes over medium-low heat, stirring occasionally.

Stir in the Romaine and parsley, and cook for 5 to 10 minutes more. To thicken the soup, mash the potatoes against the side of the pan with a wooden spoon. Remove from the heat and let sit for about 10 minutes. If you'd like, stir in the vinegar.

Ladle the soup into bowls and serve with warm bread.

Yield: 6 servings

Japanese Miso, Mizuna, and Udon Soup

This aromatic miso broth is filled with a cornucopia of shapes, textures, and colors. From daikon, kombu, and tofu to exotic mushrooms, leafy mizuna, and udon (a wheat noodle), this soup emanates the intriguing flavors of Japanese cuisine.

1	(8-inch) strip of kombu (edible seaweed)
1	tablespoon canola oil
1	medium yellow onion, diced
6	to 8 button mushrooms, sliced
4	fresh shiitake mushrooms, sliced
2	cloves garlic, minced
6	cups water or vegetable stock
2	medium carrots, peeled and sliced at an angle
1	(2-inch) section of daikon, peeled and thinly sliced
1/4	pound tofu, cut into matchstick strips
1/2	teaspoon ground black pepper
4	ounces udon noodles, snapped in half
2	cups coarsely chopped mizuna or bok choy
2	tablespoons miso paste

Soak the kombu in warm water to cover for 30 minutes to 1 hour. Drain, discarding the liquid.

In a large saucepan heat the oil. Add the onion, mushrooms, and garlic, and sauté for 5 to 7 minutes. Add the water, kombu, carrots, daikon, tofu, and black pepper, and bring to a simmer. Cook over medium heat for about 20 minutes, stirring occasionally. Remove any small foamy particles that float to the surface.

Stir in the noodles and mizuna greens. Cook for 15 to 20 minutes more over low heat.

Meanwhile, dissolve the miso paste in 2 to 3 tablespoons warm water. At the last minute, stir the miso paste into the soup. Do not boil the soup once the miso has been added. Set aside for 5 minutes. Remove the strips of kombu before serving.

Ladle the soup into large soup bowls and serve hot.

Yield: 6 servings

Soup Tips

Kombu, miso, mizuna, and udon noodles can be found at Asian grocery stores and well-stocked natural food stores. Fresh shiitake mushrooms and daikon are available in the produce sections of well-stocked grocery stores. Mizuna is sometimes available at the farmers' market.

Artichoke and White Bean Stew

Artichokes romance the palate with finesse and subtlety. Although I don't subscribe to the "less is more" theory of spicing, with an artichoke soup all that is needed is parsley, a hint of lemon, and the usual entourage of onion, celery, and garlic. A crunchy French baguette mops up the stew wonderfully.

1	tablespoon canola oil
1	medium yellow onion, diced
1	large stalk celery, chopped
2	cloves garlic, minced
6	cups water
2	medium carrots, peeled and diced
2	cups diced white potatoes
1/4	cup dry white wine
1	tablespoon dried parsley
3/4	teaspoon salt
1/2	teaspoon ground black pepper
1	(14-ounce) can artichoke hearts, drained and coarsely chopped (about 6 hearts)
1	(15-ounce) can white kidney beans (cannellini), drained
2	or 3 tablespoons chopped fresh parsley
2	lemons, quartered

In a large saucepan heat the oil. Add the onion, celery, and garlic, and sauté for 5 minutes. Add the water, carrots, potatoes, wine, and dried seasonings, and bring to a simmer. Cook over medium-low heat for about 15 minutes, stirring occasionally.

Stir in the artichokes and white beans, and cook for 15 to 20 minutes more over low heat, stirring occasionally. Stir in the parsley and squeeze half of the lemon wedges into the soup. Let the soup stand for 10 minutes before ladling into bowls.

Serve with loaves of French baguettes. Pass the extra lemon at the table.

Yield: 6 to 8 servings

Soup Tips

Artichokes packed in water have fewer calories than those packed in oil.

Curried Potato and Green Pea Soup

This soup is patterned after an Indian green pea soup called hara shorva. It can be served as a stew or bisque, depending on your preference.

1	tablespoon canola oil
1	medium yellow onion, diced
2	cloves garlic, minced
1	small serrano or cayenne pepper, seeded and minced
2	teaspoons curry powder
1	teaspoon ground cumin
1	teaspoon ground coriander
1/2	teaspoon garam masala (optional)
1/2	teaspoon salt
6	cups water
4	cups diced white potatoes (peeled, if desired)
1	large carrot, peeled and diced
2	cups frozen green peas

In a large saucepan heat the oil. Add the onion, garlic, and serrano pepper, and sauté for 4 minutes. Stir in the seasonings and cook for 1 minute more over low heat. Add the water, potatoes, and carrot, and cook over medium-low heat for 20 to 25 minutes, stirring occasionally, until the potatoes are tender. Stir in the green peas and cook for 5 to 7 minutes more over low heat. Remove from the heat and let stand for 10 minutes.

To thicken, mash some of the potatoes against the side of the pan with the back of a spoon. You may also puree the soup in a blender or food processor fitted with a steel blade and serve as a bisque.

Yield: 6 servings

Soup Tips

Cucumber Yogurt Raita (page 241), Braised Spinach Raita (page 243), or a few dollops of plain yogurt can be served as accompaniments. A squeeze of fresh lemon at the last minute is another traditional way of perking up the soup.

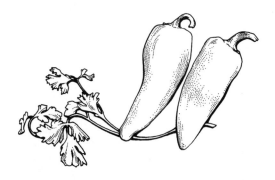

Curried Cauliflower Bisque

In all honesty, cauliflower is usually the one vegetable I consistently overlook and allow to loiter in the back of the refrigerator. But when I do take the time to cook with cauliflower—and combine it with the proper spices—I am almost always pleasantly surprised. Hope reigns eternal for cauliflower when the spice cabinet is full.

1 tablespoon canola oil
1 medium yellow onion, diced
1 celery stalk, chopped
2 cloves garlic, minced
1 small jalapeño or cayenne pepper, seeded and minced (optional)
2 teaspoons minced fresh ginger
1 large tomato, diced
2 teaspoons curry powder
1 teaspoon ground cumin
1 teaspoon ground coriander
1 teaspoon salt
1/2 teaspoon fenugreek (optional)
7 cups water
2 cups diced white potatoes (peeled, if desired)
1 medium head cauliflower, cut into florets (about a 2-pound head)

In a large saucepan heat the oil. Add the onion, celery, garlic, chile, and ginger, and sauté for 4 minutes. Stir in the tomato and seasonings, and cook for 1 minute more over low heat. Add the water, potatoes, and cauliflower, and cook over medium-low heat for 30 minutes, stirring occasionally, until the potatoes and cauliflower are tender. Remove from the heat and let stand for 10 minutes.

Transfer the soup to a blender or food processor fitted with a steel blade and puree until smooth.

Ladle into bowls and serve with a warm Indian flat bread such as nan, roti, or chapati bread.

Yield: 6 servings

Soup Tips

Serve with Cucumber Yogurt Raita (page 241), Braised Spinach Raita (page 243), or a few dollops of plain yogurt. Fenugreek is a fragrant spice available in Indian markets and well-stocked natural food stores.

Ital Stew with
Corn Dumplings

This hearty Jamaican soup is made in the Rastafarian tradition—no salt, meat, or processed foods. "Ital" refers to this practice.

For the dumplings:
1/2 cup fine cornmeal
1/2 cup unbleached all-purpose flour
1/2 teaspoon baking powder
5 to 6 tablespoons water, to bind

For the stew:
1 tablespoon canola oil
1 medium onion, diced
1 green bell pepper, seeded and diced
1 chayote squash or small zucchini, diced
2 or 3 cloves garlic, minced
6 cups water or vegetable stock
2 cups peeled and diced West Indian pumpkin
   or butternut squash
2 tablespoons dried parsley
2 teaspoons dried thyme
1/2 teaspoon ground black pepper
1 whole Scotch bonnet pepper, punctured with a
   fork (optional)
   Juice of 1 lime

To make the dumplings, combine the cornmeal, flour, and baking powder in a mixing bowl. Gradually add the water to form a moist, pliable dough. Divide the dough into 8 equal balls. Set aside until the stew is simmering.

To make the stew, heat the oil in a large saucepan. Add the onion, bell pepper, squash, and garlic, and sauté for about 7 minutes. Add the water, butternut squash, and seasonings, and bring to a simmer. Add the dumplings and Scotch bonnet pepper, and cook for 30 to 35 minutes over medium heat, stirring occasionally.

Remove the Scotch bonnet pepper from the stew, cut into strips, and give to those who love fiery hot food. Stir in the lime juice and ladle the stew into bowls, making sure everyone gets a dumpling.

Yield: 6 to 8 servings

Champagne Mushroom Soup

Whenever cream of mushroom was on the menu at my restaurant, it rapidly sold out. However, it was made with real heavy cream and it would not pass muster in today's health-conscious climate. In pursuit of a lighter version, I created this creamless mushroom soup, and sacrificed not a trace of flavor.

1 1/2 tablespoons canola oil
1   pound button mushrooms, sliced
1   medium yellow onion, diced
1   stalk celery, chopped
2   or 3 cloves garlic, minced
2   tablespoons unbleached all-purpose flour
3 1/2 cups water
1   medium white potato, peeled and diced
1/2   cup dry Champagne or white wine
3   tablespoons chopped fresh parsley (about 1/2 tablespoon dried)
1   teaspoon paprika
1/2   teaspoon salt
1/8   teaspoon ground cayenne pepper
1   cup whole or lowfat milk

In a large saucepan heat the oil. Add the mushrooms, onion, celery, and garlic, and cook for 7 to 10 minutes over medium heat, stirring occasionally. Stir in the flour and cook for 1 minute more, stirring frequently. Add the water, potato, Champagne or wine, and seasonings, and bring to a simmer. Cook for 20 to 30 minutes over medium-low heat, stirring occasionally.

To thicken, mash the potatoes against the side of the pan with the back of a spoon. Stir in the milk and bring to a gentle simmer. Remove from the heat and let stand for 5 to 10 minutes before serving.

Ladle into bowls and serve with warm dark bread.

Yield: 4 to 6 servings

Soup Tips

For a little flavor adventure, add a half dozen or so wild mushrooms such as cremini, oyster, or shiitaki in place of six or eight button mushrooms.

Hearty Vegetable Panade

Panade is a soup that is ladled over bread and left to soak. (Panade is from the French word for "bread.") The idea of soup and bread sharing the same bowl harkens back to the days when a broth was poured over a "sop," or hunk of bread. I like to pour this hearty panade over fancy jalapeño cheese bread or tantalizing Tuscan bruschetta.

2	tablespoons olive oil
1	medium red onion, diced
1	small yellow or green zucchini, diced
2	or 3 cloves garlic, minced
7	cups water
2	carrots, peeled and diced
1	medium white potato, diced (do not peel)
1	medium parsnip or turnip, peeled and diced
1	(14-ounce) can stewed tomatoes
1/4	cup dry red wine
2	teaspoons dried oregano
1	teaspoon dried basil
1/2	teaspoon salt
1/2	teaspoon ground black pepper
	About 12 slices Italian bread, French bread, or fancy cheese bread, torn into pieces
1	cup grated lowfat Swiss cheese or part-skim mozzarella cheese

In a large saucepan heat the oil. Add the onion, zucchini, and garlic, and sauté for 5 minutes. Stir in the water, carrots, potato, parsnip or turnip, stewed tomatoes, wine, and seasonings, and bring to a simmer. Cook for about 45 minutes to 1 hour over medium-low heat, stirring occasionally. Remove from the heat and let stand for 10 minutes.

Place the torn bread into the bottom of each soup bowl. Ladle the soup over the bread and pack it down with a spoon. Sprinkle the cheese over top. Let the soup sit for a few minutes, allowing the bread to soak in the broth. Pass the extra bread at the table.

Yield: 6 servings

Soup Tips
Add 2 or 3 tablespoons of chopped herbs (such as basil, oregano, marjoram, and parsley) to the soup near the finish.

Caldo Gallego
(Galician Soup)

This hearty Spanish cauldron of potatoes, turnip greens, and white beans is a close cousin to Portuguese Caldo Verde (page 31). It is a nutritious stew with a stick-to-your-ribs quality.

1	tablespoon olive oil
1	medium yellow onion, chopped
2	or 3 cloves garlic, minced
4	cups water
2	cups diced white potatoes (peeled if desired)
2	medium turnips, peeled and diced
1/2	teaspoon salt
1/2	teaspoon ground white or black pepper
2	cups chopped turnip greens or mustard greens
1	(15-ounce) can white kidney beans (cannellini), drained
1/4	cup minced fresh parsley

In a large saucepan heat the oil. Add the onion and garlic, and sauté for about 4 minutes. Add the water, potatoes, turnips, and dried seasonings, and cook for 20 to 25 minutes over medium heat, stirring occasionally. Stir in the turnip greens, beans, and parsley, and cook for 10 to 15 minutes more. Turn off the heat and let stand for about 10 minutes. To thicken, mash the potatoes against the side of the pan with the back of a spoon.

Ladle the soup into bowls and serve with warm crusty bread.

Yield: 6 servings

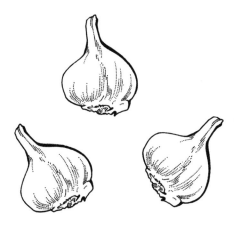

Emily's Asparagus Vichyssoise

Asparagus is a regal vegetable with a distinctive flavor reminiscent of broccoli and corn. My friend Emily Robin, who is quite a fancier of asparagus, gave me the idea for this tasty improvisation on vichyssoise.

1   tablespoon canola oil
1   medium yellow onion, diced
2   cups rinsed and coarsely chopped leeks
2   cloves garlic, minced
4   cups water
2   cups peeled and coarsely chopped white potatoes
1/2 teaspoon ground white pepper
1/2 teaspoon salt
12   asparagus spears, trimmed and cut into 1/2-inch
     pieces (about 2 cups)
1 1/2 cups lowfat or whole milk
1/4 cup chopped whole parsley
1   lemon, quartered
2   tablespoons chopped fresh chives (for garnish)

In a large saucepan heat the oil. Add the onion, leeks, and garlic, and sauté for 5 to 7 minutes, until the vegetables are tender. Add the water, potatoes, and dried seasonings, and bring to a simmer. Cook over medium-low heat for about 15 minutes, stirring occasionally. Stir in the asparagus and cook for 10 minutes more.

Stir in the milk and parsley and return briefly to a gentle simmer. Remove from the heat and squeeze the lemon into the soup; let cool for a few minutes.

Transfer the soup to a blender or food processor fitted with a steel blade and puree until smooth. Ladle into bowls and serve hot, or chill for later. Sprinkle chives over the soup before serving.

Yield: 6 servings

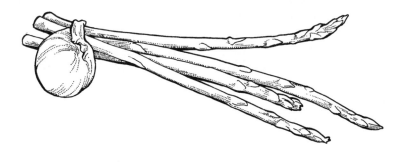

Cheddar Broccoli and Winter Squash Bisque

What is it about cheddar and broccoli soups that stokes the appetite? The two share a great affinity for each other. This version is enriched with butternut squash and celery-like broccoli stalks. A pinch of nutmeg imbues the bisque with a faint, but familiar accent.

1	tablespoon canola oil
1	medium yellow onion, diced
1	cup chopped broccoli stalk
2	or 3 cloves garlic, minced
2	cups peeled and diced butternut or other winter squash
4	cups water
1 1/2	tablespoons dried parsley
1/2	teaspoon salt
1/2	teaspoon ground white pepper
1/4	teaspoon ground nutmeg
1	medium bunch broccoli, cut into florets
1	to 1 1/2 cups whole or lowfat milk
1	cup shredded sharp cheddar cheese (preferably lowfat)

In a large saucepan heat the oil. Add the onion, broccoli stalks, and garlic, and sauté for about 5 minutes. Add the squash, water, and seasonings, and bring to a simmer. Cook for about 20 minutes over medium-low heat, stirring occasionally. Stir in the broccoli florets, and cook for 8 to 10 minutes more until the broccoli is tender. Stir in the milk and remove from the heat; let the soup cool slightly.

Transfer the soup to a blender or food processor fitted with a steel blade and process for about 10 seconds, until smooth. Return to the pan and blend in the cheese.

Ladle into bowls and serve with warm French bread.

Yield: 6 to 8 servings

Lemony Lentil Soup
with Bulgur Dumplings

*This brothy Middle Eastern soup was a Sunday staple in
Myers Heights, a small bucolic village near Ithaca, New
York, where my father grew up. The broth is saturated with
lentils, vegetables, bulgur wheat dumplings, and noodles—a
meal by itself. The robust soup is finessed by a last-minute
surge of fresh-squeezed lemon.*

1	tablespoon canola oil
1	medium yellow onion, diced
2	stalks celery, chopped
1	small cousa or yellow summer squash, diced
2	cloves garlic, minced
8	cups hot water or vegetable stock
3	or 4 medium carrots, peeled and diced
1/2	cup green lentils, rinsed
1/2	teaspoon ground cumin (optional)
1/2	teaspoon ground black pepper
2	to 4 ounces egg noodles or linguini
8	to 12 bulgur dumplings (see recipe)
	Juice of 2 lemons
1/2	teaspoon salt

In a large saucepan heat the oil. Add the onion, celery,
cousa, and garlic, and sauté for 5 to 7 minutes. Stir in the
water, carrots, lentils, cumin, and black pepper, and bring to
a boil. Cook over medium-low heat for 30 to 40 minutes,
stirring occasionally.

Stir in the noodles, bulgur dumplings, lemon juice, and salt, and cook for 10 to 15 minutes over low heat.

To serve, place a dumpling in each soup bowl and ladle the soup over the top.

Yield: 6 to 8 servings

Bulgur Dumplings

1	cup bulgur (fine cracked wheat)
1/4	cup all-purpose flour
1/2	teaspoon salt
2	to 3 tablespoons chopped fresh parsley
1	large egg, beaten
2	to 3 tablespoons water

In a medium mixing bowl combine the bulgur, flour, salt, and parsley. Blend in the egg and water to form a moist ball. Divide the dough and roll into 6 to 8 small golf ball–shaped dumplings. Cover and refrigerate for about 15 minutes.

When the soup is ready, gently drop the dumplings into the simmering soup and cook for 10 to 15 minutes more, stirring occasionally.

Soup Tips

Cousa is a pale green summer squash with a firm white flesh. Bulgur is available in natural food stores, well-stocked supermarkets, and ethnic markets.

Red Lentil and Barley Stew

This satisfying legume and grain stew radiates with the comforting presence of ginger, cumin, and turmeric.

1	tablespoon canola oil
1	large yellow onion, diced
2	stalks celery, diced
2	teaspoons minced fresh ginger
1 1/2	teaspoons ground cumin
1	teaspoon ground coriander
1/2	teaspoon turmeric
1/4	teaspoon cayenne pepper
8	cups water
1	cup red lentils, rinsed
1/2	cup pearl barley
2	medium white potatoes, diced (peeled if desired)
1	teaspoon salt
	Juice of 1 lemon

In a large saucepan heat the oil. Add the onion, celery, and ginger, and sauté for 5 minutes. Stir in all of the seasonings (except the salt) and cook for 30 seconds more. Stir in the water, lentils, barley, and potatoes, and bring to a simmer. Cook over medium-low heat for about 1 hour, stirring occasionally.

Remove from the heat and stir in the salt and lemon juice. Let stand for 5 to 10 minutes before serving.

Ladle the stew into bowls and serve with warm bread.

Yield: 6 to 8 servings

Soup Tips

Add 2 medium carrots, peeled and diced, along with the potatoes or stir in 2 cups of chopped kale or spinach about 10 minutes before the stew has finished cooking. Red lentils are available at natural food stores and well-stocked supermarkets.

Chapter 6

Summery Bowls and Fruity Bisques

The summer menu heralds a smorgasbord of light soups and bisques with refined flavors and textures. Whether serving a chilled fruit bisque or hot broth of noodles and garden vegetables, iridescent summer soups quench the appetite while replenishing one's energy. A bowl of soup accompanied by fresh bread and tossed green salad makes for a pleasing and satisfying solstice meal under the sun.

The summer pantry expands beyond the traditional hardy soup staples. Naturally sweet and succulent fruits such as berries, melons, peaches, and mangoes inspire a medley of chilled soup creations. Cherry Apricot Bisque, Blueberry Bisque with Mango Puree, Calypso Fruit Bisque, Cool Cucumber Bisque, and many other inspirations from the fruit orchards make delightful first courses or winsome finales.

Not to be forgotten, a harvest of vegetables—tomatoes, green beans, summer squash, and eggplant—is in abundant supply. This chapter features summer classics such as Master Gardener's Country Stew, Roasted Garlic and Yellow Squash Chowder, and Portuguese Green Bean Tureen. Fresh garden herbs—basil, oregano, mint, and parsley—are omnipresent and omniflavorful.

There are several enticing renditions of gazpacho, the classic chilled soup rooted in Spanish cuisine. The "liquid salad" of raw vegetables, herbs, and liquified tomatoes is naturally healthful, loaded with flavor, and easy to prepare. This chapter includes the traditional Andalusian Gazpacho along with an innovative Gardenfest Gazpacho, an adventurous Grilled and Chilled Vegetable Soup, and other exciting variations.

A Master Gardener's Country Stew

Recently I completed a master gardening course sponsored by the local cooperative extension. While most of the students focused on perennial and ornamental flowers, I dreamed of Godzilla eggplants, killer tomatoes, monster squash, and a jungle of chile peppers. The training paid off—my blooming garden inspired this robust stew.

2	tablespoons canola oil
1	medium yellow onion, diced
1	Japanese eggplant, diced (about 1 1/2 cups)
1	medium yellow or green zucchini, diced
1	green or red bell pepper, seeded and diced
2	or 3 cloves garlic, minced
1	cayenne or red jalapeño pepper, seeded and minced (optional)
2	large ripe tomatoes, diced
4	cups water or vegetable stock
1/4	cup tomato paste
2	teaspoons dried oregano
1/2	teaspoon ground black pepper
1/2	teaspoon salt
1/3	cup orzo or small soup shells
1/4	pound green beans, trimmed and cut into 1/2-inch sections
3	or 4 tablespoons chopped fresh parsley
2	or 3 tablespoons chopped fresh basil

Vegetarian Soup Cuisine

In a large saucepan heat the oil. Add the onion, eggplant, zucchini, bell pepper, garlic, and chile pepper, and cook for 8 to 10 minutes over medium heat, stirring frequently. Stir in the tomatoes and cook for about 3 to 4 minutes more over low heat. Stir in the water, tomato paste, and dried seasonings, and bring to a simmer. Cook over medium-low heat for about 10 minutes, stirring occasionally.

Stir in the pasta and green beans, and cook for 12 to 15 minutes more. Stir in the fresh herbs and let stand for 10 minutes before serving.

Ladle into bowls and serve with whole grain bread and a carafe of red wine.

Yield: 6 servings

Roasted Sweet Corn and Sweet Potato Chowder

The sight of corn-on-the-cob roasting on the grill could be the universal symbol for summer. I like to barbecue extra ears of corn and make soup with the leftovers the following day. This is yet another healthful rendition of chowder. "Chowder" is from the French word chaudière, a large cauldron or kettle.

4	ears of corn-on-the-cob, unshucked
1	tablespoon canola oil
1	medium yellow onion, diced
1	red or green bell pepper, seeded and diced
1	cup sliced celery
2	cloves garlic, minced
6	cups water
4	cups diced sweet potatoes
2	teaspoons dried oregano
1	teaspoon salt
1 1/2	teaspoons dried thyme leaves
1/2	teaspoon ground black pepper
1 1/2	cups whole or lowfat milk
2	to 3 tablespoons chopped fresh parsley

Soak the corn in a large pot or pail of water for 15 to 20 minutes. Drain and shake off any excess water.

Preheat the grill until the coals are ashen gray to white. Place the corn on the grill and cook for 15 minutes, turning every 4 minutes or so. When the husks are slightly charred, remove from the heat and let cool slightly. Shuck the corn and rinse the ears under running water. With a sharp knife cut the corn kernels off the cob. Refrigerate the corn until ready to use.

In a large saucepan heat the oil. Add the onion, bell pepper, celery, and garlic, and sauté for 5 to 7 minutes. Add the water, sweet potatoes, and dried seasonings, and bring to a simmer. Cook for 15 minutes over low heat, stirring occasionally.

Stir in the corn and cook for 10 to 15 minutes more. Stir in the milk and parsley, and return to a gentle simmer. To thicken, ladle 1 or 2 cups of the soup into a food processor fitted with a steel blade or a blender and process until smooth. Return the puree to the soup and restore to a simmer.

Ladle the chowder into bowls and serve hot.

Yield: 8 servings

Soup Tips

If in season, add one or two roasted poblano or New Mexico chiles (seeded and diced) to the chowder for a piquant nuance.

Garden Gumbo

In the annals of soup cookery, gumbo must go down as one of the most spirited and adventurous offerings. Just about anything goes into a gumbo. However, there is one constant: onion, bell pepper, and celery (the "holy trinity" of Cajun cooking) form the classic foundation. This meatless version is chock-full of garden vegetables, brown rice, and red beans.

1	tablespoon canola oil
1	medium yellow onion, diced
1	yellow or red bell pepper, seeded and diced
1	small zucchini, diced
1	stalk celery, sliced
2	or 3 cloves garlic, minced
6	cups water or vegetable stock
1	(14-ounce) can stewed tomatoes
1/2	cup long grain brown rice
2	teaspoons dried oregano
1 1/2	teaspoons dried thyme
1	teaspoon salt
1/4	teaspoon ground black pepper
1/4	teaspoon ground cayenne pepper
1/4	cup chopped fresh parsley
1	(15-ounce) can red kidney beans, drained

In a large saucepan heat the oil. Add the onion, bell pepper, zucchini, celery, and garlic, and cook for 7 to 9 minutes over medium heat, stirring frequently. Stir in the water, stewed tomatoes, rice, and dried seasonings, and cook over low heat for 45 to 50 minutes, stirring occasionally. Stir in the parsley and beans and cook for 5 to 10 minutes more.

Let the gumbo stand for 10 to 15 minutes before serving. Serve with Quintessential Corn Bread (page 239), and pass a bottle of Tabasco sauce at the table.

Yield: 8 servings

Gardenfest Gazpacho

Gazpacho is almost synonymous with summer. The chilled soup is to July what chili is to January. This nourishing version is culled from a well-cultivated vegetable garden (or local farmers' market).

2	medium ripe tomatoes, diced
1	small red onion, diced
1	medium green or red bell pepper, seeded and diced
1	medium cucumber, peeled and diced
1	or 2 cloves garlic, minced
1	small serrano or cayenne pepper, seeded and minced (optional)
1/4	cup chopped fresh parsley
1/2	teaspoon Tabasco or other hot sauce
1/2	teaspoon ground black pepper
1/2	teaspoon salt
2	cups canned tomato juice or V-8 juice
2	tablespoons chopped fresh basil (optional)

Combine all of the ingredients in a large mixing bowl and blend thoroughly. Transfer about three-quarters of the mixture to a blender or food processor fitted with a steel blade; process for 5 seconds. Return the pureed mixture to the mixing bowl and blend with the remaining vegetables. Refrigerate the gazpacho for at least 2 hours before serving.

Serve the gazpacho in chilled bowls and garnish with sprigs of herbs.

Yield: 4 servings

Minty Cantaloupe Bisque

I wouldn't go so far as to call myself a juice fanatic, but I do indulge in fresh homemade juice almost every day. So it was a given that there would be at least one soup recipe from my venerable juice machine. This cool bisque is intended to be a simple palate refresher. "Melon alone or leave it alone," my father is fond of saying.

1	large ripe cantaloupe
1	cup lowfat plain yogurt
6	to 8 fresh mint leaves cut into thin strips (chiffonade style)
1/4	teaspoon ground nutmeg

Cut the cantaloupe in half and scoop out the seeds. Scrub or pare the skin off and slice the cantaloupe into thin wedges. Place the wedges one by one into the juice extractor. (If using a blender or food processor fitted with a steel blade, completely peel and dice up the cantaloupe; puree until smooth.) There should be about 3 cups. Pour the pureed cantaloupe into a bowl.

Whisk the yogurt and mint into the cantaloupe. Pour the soup into chilled bowls and serve immediately, or refrigerate for 1 hour. Sprinkle the nutmeg over the top before serving.

Yield: 4 servings

Grilled and Chilled Vegetable Soup

This smoky, chunky cold soup captures the outdoorsy and adventurous spirit of summer and brings a taste of the grill to the soup bowl. You can grill the vegetables a day ahead and refrigerate for later use. This soup is also a good way to use up leftover grilled veggies.

2	plum tomatoes
1	small red onion, peeled and halved
1	medium green or red bell pepper
1	medium zucchini, cut widthwise into 1/2-inch ovals
1	small eggplant, cut widthwise into 1/2-inch ovals
2	cloves garlic, minced
2	tablespoons chopped fresh parsley
1/2	teaspoon ground black pepper
1/2	teaspoon salt
3	cups canned tomato juice

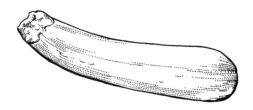

Preheat the grill until the coals are gray to white.

When the fire is ready, place the vegetables on the lightly oiled grill. Cook the vegetables for 5 to 7 minutes on each side, until they become tender and develop grill marks. Using tongs or a spatula, remove the vegetables to a large mixing bowl as they become done.

After the vegetables have cooled slightly, remove any charred spots and discard. Peel (or rub) off the skin of the bell pepper; discard the core and seeds. Chop all of the vegetables and place in a medium mixing bowl. Add the remaining ingredients and blend thoroughly. Refrigerate the gazpacho for at least 2 hours, preferably overnight.

Serve in chilled bowls and garnish with sprigs of herbs.

Yield: 6 servings

Soup Tips

To punch up the flavors a bit, add 2 tablespoons chopped fresh cilantro, basil, or mint. If poblano or New Mexico chiles are available, grill along with the vegetables. (Peel the skin and remove the seeds before adding to the gazpacho.)

Farmers' Market Vegetable Pot

*This soup highlights the bountiful harvest found at farmers'
markets around the country. The farmers' markets are home
to exotic leafy greens, vibrant herbs like opal basil, juicy
vine-ripened tomatoes, and colorful potatoes and peppers. I
am always inspired and rejuvenated after a visit.*

1	tablespoon canola oil
1	medium red onion, diced
1	red or yellow bell pepper, seeded and diced
2	plum tomatoes, diced
1	cup rinsed and coarsely chopped leeks
1	Red Fresno or red jalapeño pepper, seeded and minced (optional)
6	cups water
2	cups diced red or blue potatoes (peeled if desired)
1/2	cup garlic greens, chopped
1/2	teaspoon salt
1/2	teaspoon ground black pepper
2	cups coarsely chopped red Russian kale or red chard
2	to 3 tablespoons chopped fresh parsley
2	tablespoons chopped opal (purple) basil or sweet basil

In a large saucepan heat the oil. Add the onion, bell pepper, tomatoes, leeks, and chile, and sauté for 5 to 7 minutes. Add the water, potatoes, garlic greens, and dried seasonings, and bring to a simmer. Cook for 20 to 25 minutes over medium-low heat, stirring occasionally, until the potatoes are tender.

Stir in the kale and cook for 10 minutes more. Stir in the fresh herbs and remove from the heat; let stand for about 10 minutes before serving.

Ladle the soup into bowls and serve with warm crusty bread.

Yield: 6 servings

Soup Tips

The perfect accompaniment for this soup: hearth-style bread slathered with soft goat cheese. Feel free to add other fresh herbs, such as oregano, marjoram, or arugula along with (or in place of) the parsley and basil. Other market greens, such as frisee, mizuna, and baby bok choy (*pat soi*) may also be added.

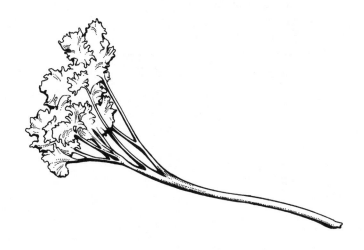

Wild Grape Leaf
and Rice Soup

*Vines of wild grape leaves grow with reckless abandon in
northern parts of the country, especially where I live in
upstate New York. Although the grape leaves (also called
vine leaves) are better known as the wrapping for dolmades,
the Greek and Middle Eastern stuffed delicacy, they also
make flavorful soup greens.*

1	tablespoon canola oil
1	medium yellow onion, diced
1	small zucchini, diced
2	cloves garlic, minced
6	cups water
1	(14-ounce) can stewed tomatoes
2	cups grape leaves (chiffonade style)
1	(15-ounce) can chickpeas, drained
1/3	cup long grain white rice or converted rice
3	tablespoons tomato paste
1 1/2	tablespoons dried parsley
1	teaspoon salt
1/2	teaspoon ground black pepper
	Juice of 1 lemon (optional)

In a large saucepan heat the oil. Add the onion, zucchini, and garlic, and sauté for 5 to 7 minutes. Add the water, stewed tomatoes, grape leaves, chickpeas, rice, tomato paste, and seasonings, and bring to a simmer. Cook for about 25 minutes over low heat, stirring occasionally.

Let the soup stand for a few minutes before serving. If desired, stir in the lemon juice. Ladle into bowls and serve with warm pita bread.

Yield: 6 to 8 servings

Soup Tips

Cut the leaves chiffonade style by rolling them up and cutting into thin ribbons. If grape leaves are unavailable in your area, red or green chard or beet greens may be substituted.

Blueberry Bisque with Mango Puree

This refreshing soup is as appealing to the eye as it is to the palate. The fruity bisque of tangy, plump blueberries is heightened with a touch of honey and a tropical puree of luscious mangoes. Look for ripe, soft-when-pressed mangoes that have a fragrant aroma.

For the mango puree:
2 ripe mangoes, peeled, pitted, and diced
2 cups plain lowfat yogurt
1/2 cup lowfat milk or vanilla soy milk

For the blueberry bisque:
3 cups blueberries, rinsed
1 cup plain lowfat yogurt
1/2 cup lowfat milk, whole milk, or soy milk
1 1/2 tablespoons honey
2 tablespoons chopped fresh mint (optional)

Combine the mango, yogurt, and milk in a blender, and blend for 5 to 10 seconds until smooth. Transfer to a serving bowl and rinse the blender.

Combine the blueberries, yogurt, milk, and honey in the blender, and blend for 5 to 10 seconds until smooth. Transfer to a serving bowl. To serve, ladle the blueberry bisque into chilled soup bowls, filling about halfway. Swirl the mango puree over the top. If desired, sprinkle the mint.

Yield: 4 servings

Peach Orchard Soup

A succulent, tree-ripened peach can be a wonderful, beautiful thing. A sign advertising ripe summer peaches for sale will stop me in my tracks every time. For this inventive chilled soup, peaches are first poached in apple juice, and then pureed into a light and sweet summertime bisque.

4	large ripe peaches, pitted and diced
2	cups apple juice
1	tablespoon dark rum
1/4	teaspoon ground nutmeg
1	cup plain lowfat yogurt
1	tablespoon honey
2	tablespoons chopped fresh mint (optional)
1	peach, pitted and cut into thin wedges

In a medium saucepan combine the diced peaches, apple juice, rum, and nutmeg. Bring to a simmer and cook over low heat for about 10 minutes, stirring occasionally. Remove from the heat and let cool slightly. Pour the fruit mixture into a blender and blend for 5 to 10 seconds until smooth. Refrigerate for about 2 hours.

Transfer the chilled peach puree to a mixing bowl and blend in the yogurt and honey.

To serve, ladle the soup into chilled soup bowls. If desired, sprinkle the mint over the top and garnish with fanned peach slices.

Yield: 4 to 6 servings

Soup Tips
For a Peach and Plum Bisque, poach two plums (pitted and diced) in place of one of the peaches.

Potato and Leek Vichyssoise with Buttermilk

Buttermilk is lower in fat than milk or cream and gives this classic potato and leek bisque a lemony tang. Considering that traditional vichyssoise is laden with heavy cream—the same kind of cream used for ice cream—this version is as good for your heart as it is for your palate. Dill adds an herbal accent at the finish.

1	tablespoon canola oil
1	medium yellow onion, diced
2	cups rinsed and chopped leeks
2	cloves garlic, minced
4	cups water
4	cups peeled and coarsely chopped white potatoes
1/4	cup dry white wine
1 1/2	tablespoons dried parsley
1/2	teaspoon salt
1/2	teaspoon ground white pepper
2	cups buttermilk
1	medium cucumber, peeled and chopped
2	tablespoons chopped fresh dill

In a large saucepan heat the oil. Add the onion, leeks, and garlic, and sauté for about 5 minutes. Add the water, potatoes, wine, and dried seasonings, and bring to a simmer. Cook over low heat for about 25 minutes, stirring occasionally. Stir in the buttermilk, cucumber, and dill, and cook for about 30 seconds more. Remove the soup from the heat and let cool slightly. Transfer the soup to a blender or food processor fitted with a steel blade and puree until smooth.

Ladle into bowls and serve immediately, or chill for later. Serve with a warm French baguette.

Yield: 6 to 8 servings

Vegetarian Soup Cuisine

Cool Cucumber Bisque

From out of my past comes this savory soup. Many years ago I served it as a summer special at my first restaurant. While most cucumber bisques include raw cucumbers, this version calls for an initial sautéing of the cucumbers, onion, and garlic. Once again, heavy cream has been replaced by lowfat milk and yogurt.

1	tablespoon canola oil
1	medium yellow onion, diced
2	cloves garlic, minced
2	large cucumbers, peeled and diced
1 1/2	cups whole or lowfat milk
1/2	cup plain lowfat yogurt
2	tablespoons chopped fresh parsley
1	to 2 tablespoons chopped fresh dill
1/2	teaspoon salt
1/2	teaspoon ground white pepper

In a medium saucepan heat the oil. Add the onion and garlic, and sauté for 4 minutes. Add the cucumbers and sauté for 3 minutes more. Stir in the milk, yogurt, and seasonings, and bring to a gentle simmer. Remove from the heat and let cool slightly.

Transfer the soup to a blender or food processor fitted with a steel blade and puree until smooth. Refrigerate for 2 to 4 hours before serving.

Serve with crusty loaves of French baguettes.

Yield: 6 servings

Hawaiian Papaya Soup

This mellow blend of tropical papayas and nutty coconut was inspired by a visit to balmy Hawaii. The lush islands may be famous for sunny skies and pristine beaches, but there is also a burgeoning culinary renaissance underway. No longer dependent on imported goods, today's island chefs have developed a regional cuisine promoting (and using) locally grown ingredients.

2	ripe papayas, peeled, seeded, and chopped
1	cup lowfat coconut milk or vanilla soy milk
1	cup whole or lowfat milk
1	tablespoon dark rum
1	tablespoon honey
	Juice of 1 lime
4	to 6 mint leaves, cut into ribbons (for garnish)

Place all of the ingredients (except the mint) in a blender or food processor fitted with a steel blade and process for 5 to 10 seconds until smooth. Transfer to a storage bowl and refrigerate for at least 1 hour before serving.

Ladle the soup into chilled bowls and garnish with the mint leaves.

Yield: 3 or 4 servings

Soup Tips

Papayas and coconut milk are available in well-stocked grocery stores and Asian or Latin American markets.

Calypso Fruit Soup

From the Caribbean to the Pacific, there is a bounty of luscious fruit: mangoes, coral papayas, quenching star fruits, and tangy kiwis. When pureed and accented with island-grown spices (such as nutmeg and allspice), tropical soups bring a delightful sensation to the taste buds.

1	ripe mango, peeled, pitted, and diced
1	ripe papaya, seeded, scooped, and chopped
1	large kiwi fruit, peeled and diced
1	cup lowfat coconut milk or vanilla soy milk
1	to 1 1/2 cups whole or lowfat milk
2	tablespoons dark rum
1	tablespoon honey
1/4	teaspoon ground nutmeg
1/4	teaspoon ground allspice
1	star fruit, sliced widthwise (for garnish)

Place all of the ingredients (except the star fruit) in a blender or food processor fitted with a steel blade and process for 5 to 10 seconds until smooth. Transfer to a storage bowl and refrigerate for at least 1 hour before serving.

Ladle into chilled bowls and garnish with slices of star fruit.

Yield: 4 servings

Soup Tips

The best way to deal with a mango is to peel it like a potato, then cut around its large inner pit, chopping the flesh. For a papaya, cut the fruit in half lengthwise, scoop out and discard the black seeds, scoop out the flesh, and chop.

Cherry Apricot Bisque

Happiness is a bowl of cherries. I usually buy double or triple the amount of cherries needed for this recipe. For every cherry that is destined for the soup, two are eaten on the spot. Apricots, another favorite treat, add a hint of peachlike fruitiness. For this healthful soup, the fruits are first simmered in apple juice, lightly spiced, and then pureed.

6	to 8 fresh ripe apricots, pitted and diced
1/2	pound sweet cherries, pitted and halved
2	cups apple juice
2	to 3 tablespoons honey
1/4	teaspoon ground nutmeg
	Juice of 1 lime
1	cup whole or lowfat milk or vanilla soy milk
8	or 10 cherries, pitted and halved (optional garnish)

In a medium saucepan combine the apricots, cherries, and apple juice. Bring to a simmer and cook over low heat for 7 minutes, stirring occasionally. Remove from the heat and stir in the honey, nutmeg, and lime juice; let cool slightly. Pour the fruit mixture into a blender and blend for 5 to 10 seconds until smooth. Refrigerate for 2 to 4 hours.

Transfer the fruit puree to a mixing bowl and blend in the milk. To serve, ladle the soup into chilled bowls. If desired, garnish with remaining cherries.

Yield: 4 servings

Portuguese Green Bean Tureen

Green beans are forever playing second fiddle—always a secondary ingredient, never the star. Well, in this Portuguese country soup, green beans are elevated to center stage.

1	tablespoon olive oil
1	medium yellow onion, chopped
2	cloves garlic, minced
4	cups water
2	cups diced white potatoes (peeled if desired)
1/2	teaspoon salt
1/2	teaspoon ground white or black pepper
2	cups green beans, trimmed and cut into 1/2-inch sections (about 1/2 pound)
2	tablespoons chopped fresh cilantro
2	tablespoons chopped fresh parsley

In a large saucepan heat the oil. Add the onion and garlic, and sauté for about 4 minutes. Add the water, potatoes, and dried seasonings, and bring to a simmer. Cook for 20 minutes over medium heat, stirring occasionally. Stir in the green beans and cook for 10 to 15 minutes more. Turn off the heat and stir in the fresh herbs; let stand for about 10 minutes.

Pour the soup into a blender or food processor fitted with a steel blade and process for 5 to 10 seconds until smooth.

Ladle the soup into bowls and serve with warm crusty bread.

Yield: 4 servings

Soup Tips
I like to make this tureen with purple wax beans—they turn olive green when cooked.

Roasted Garlic and Yellow Squash Chowder

Roasted garlic has a smoldering, penetrating quality to it. When added to a soup or chowder, the "stinking rose" asserts its presence but does not risk overwhelming the broth. This is a soup you'll want to soak up with plenty of bread.

1	bunch garlic
1	tablespoon olive oil
1	medium yellow onion, diced
1	medium yellow zucchini or summer squash, cut in half lengthwise and sliced
1	red or green bell pepper, seeded and diced
4	cups water
2	medium white potatoes, diced (peeled if desired)
1	medium carrot, peeled and diced
1	teaspoon dried thyme
1/2	teaspoon ground black pepper
1/2	teaspoon salt
1	cup corn kernels, fresh or frozen
2	tablespoons chopped fresh parsley
1 1/2	cups whole or lowfat milk

Preheat the oven to 350°F.

Wrap the whole head of garlic in tinfoil and place in the oven. Bake for 30 to 35 minutes. Remove the garlic from the oven and unwrap; let cool to room temperature. Peel off the skin from the cloves. Mince 4 to 6 cloves; save the rest for another use.

In a large saucepan heat the oil. Add the onion, squash, and bell pepper, and sauté for 5 to 7 minutes. Stir in the garlic, water, potatoes, carrot, and dried seasonings, and bring to a simmer. Cook for 20 minutes over low heat, stirring occasionally. Stir in the corn and parsley and cook for 5 to 10 minutes more. Stir in the milk, return to a gentle simmer, and remove from the heat. To thicken, mash some of the potatoes against the side of the pan with the back of a spoon. Let sit for about 10 minutes before serving.

Ladle the chowder into warm bowls and serve with Italian bread.

Yield: 6 servings

Soup Tips

For an herbal variation, add 2 tablespoons chopped fresh basil. To fill out the color spectrum of this soup, add 2 or 3 tablespoons of roasted and diced sweet peppers or pimentos (from the jar) near the finish.

Couscous Gazpacho

Whenever I visit my brother Greg in the summer we roll out the Ping Pong table and play ferociously for hours under the sun until one of us drops or breaks a paddle; it's a competition thing. Afterward, we indulge in a refreshing gazpacho soup meal prepared from his garden. This "liquid salad" is one of my favorites.

1/2	cup couscous
3/4	cup boiling water
2	large ripe tomatoes, diced
1	small onion, diced
1	medium green or red bell pepper, seeded and diced
1	medium cucumber, peeled and diced
1	small jalapeño or serrano pepper, seeded and minced (optional)
2	cloves garlic, minced
1/4	cup chopped fresh parsley
2	to 4 tablespoons chopped fresh basil
1	teaspoon Tabasco or other bottled hot sauce
1	teaspoon ground cumin (optional)
1/4	teaspoon ground black pepper
1/4	teaspoon salt
2	cups canned tomato juice
	Assorted fresh herbs (for garnish)

In a small saucepan or bowl combine the couscous and boiling water; cover and set aside for 10 minutes.

In a large mixing bowl combine the remaining ingredients. Place three-quarters of the mixture in a blender or food processor fitted with a steel blade and process for 5 seconds, forming a vegetable mash. Return to the bowl and blend with the remaining vegetables and couscous. Chill for 30 minutes to 1 hour before serving.

Ladle the gazpacho into chilled bowls and garnish with sprigs of fresh basil or parsley. Serve with French or Italian bread.

Yield: 4 to 6 servings

Pappa al Pomodoro

This soup contains four of the ingredients held dearest to the hearts of Italian cooks: garlic, tomatoes, basil, and bread. Pappa al pomodoro ("tomato bread soup") is an old-fashioned soup saturated with garden tomatoes and spiked with basil. The soup is a simple, yet immensely pleasurable, summertime meal.

2	tablespoons olive oil
4	cloves garlic, minced
4	large ripe tomatoes, diced
1/2	teaspoon salt
1/4	teaspoon red pepper flakes
2	cups hot water
4	to 6 slices firm textured Italian bread, cut into 1/2-inch cubes
2	tablespoons fresh basil, cut into ribbons (chiffonade style)
	About 1/4 cup grated Parmesan or Romano cheese (optional)

In a large saucepan heat the oil. Add the garlic and sauté for 2 minutes. Stir in the tomatoes, salt, and red pepper, and cook for about 15 minutes over medium-low heat, stirring occasionally. Stir in the water and bread, and cook for 15 minutes more over low heat, stirring occasionally. Remove from the heat and stir in the basil. Set aside for 15 to 20 minutes, if you can wait that long.

Ladle into bowls and serve warm. If desired, sprinkle a little Parmesan or Romano cheese over the top.

Yield: 4 servings

Mediterranean Garlic and Bread Soup (Sopa de Ajo)

This garlic lover's soup (called sopa de ajo in Spanish) will permeate your kitchen with the strong characteristic scent of the beloved bulbous herb. Eggs drizzled in near the finish provide a viscous, silky texture.

2	tablespoons olive oil
4	to 6 cloves garlic, minced
4	cups trimmed and cubed French or Italian bread (about 6 slices)
6	cups water
1	teaspoon paprika
1	teaspoon salt
1/4	teaspoon cayenne pepper
2	eggs, beaten
2	tablespoons chopped fresh parsley
1	tablespoon chopped fresh cilantro

In a large saucepan heat the oil. Add the garlic and sauté for about 1 minute. Stir in the bread and cook over medium heat for 3 to 4 minutes until the bread is slightly toasted. Pour in the water and dried seasonings, and bring to a simmer. Cook for 15 minutes over low heat, stirring occasionally.

Mash the bread against the side of the pan until pulverized. Slowly drizzle in the eggs and bring to a gentle simmer (but do not boil) for about 1 minute. Stir in the herbs.

Ladle the soup into bowls and serve hot or warm.

Yield: 6 servings

Andalusian Gazpacho

While there are myriad versions of gazpacho, this recipe is rooted in the original home of the chilled summer classic: Spain. Summer vegetables and cubed bread provide the body while vinegar and cayenne pepper contribute a trace of heat.

4	ripe tomatoes, diced
1	cucumber, peeled and chopped
1	small yellow onion, diced
1	medium green bell pepper, seeded and diced
2	cloves garlic, minced
2	cups trimmed and coarsely chopped French or Italian bread
1	cup tomato juice
4	tablespoons red wine vinegar
2	tablespoons olive oil
1	teaspoon salt
1/4	teaspoon ground cayenne pepper
1/4	cup chopped fresh parsley

Combine all of the ingredients (except the parsley) in a large mixing bowl and blend thoroughly. Transfer to a blender or food processor fitted with a steel blade and process for 5 to 10 seconds until pureed. Refrigerate the gazpacho for at least 2 hours, preferably overnight.

Serve the gazpacho in chilled bowls and top with the parsley.

Yield: 6 servings

Soup Tips

It is a Spanish tradition to accompany gazpacho with bowls of chopped cucumbers, tomatoes, bell peppers, and croutons.

Key West Sunset Avocado Bisque

After meeting at a dock for a magnificent sunset on Key West, Emily and I strolled into the funky village and discovered an equally pleasurable (and rich) avocado soup at an outdoor café. This is my faithful adaptation.

4	ripe avocados, peeled, pitted, and chopped
1	papaya, peeled, seeded, and chopped
1	small tomato, diced
1	small red onion, chopped
1	clove garlic, minced
1	small cucumber, peeled and chopped
2	cups lowfat plain yogurt
1/2	teaspoon ground cumin
1/2	teaspoon ground white pepper
1/2	teaspoon salt
2	or 3 tablespoons chopped fresh parsley (for garnish)

Combine all of the ingredients in a blender or food processor fitted with a steel blade and puree until smooth.

Ladle into bowls and serve immediately or chill for later. Sprinkle the parsley over the top just before serving. Serve with warm flour tortillas and Jicama Tomato Salsa (page 252).

Yield: 6 to 8 servings

Chapter 7

Soup
Garnishes and
Accompaniments

Bread is the ultimate soup companion. Soup and bread go hand in hand, like pasta and pesto, burritos and salsa, cookies and milk. Serve a well-made soup with warm, crusty bread, and you have a recipe for happiness. Soup and bread form a simple yet divine union.

In addition to bread, of course, there are several splendid garnishes and accompaniments for soups and stews. This chapter offers a hit parade of soup companions culled from all over the world. Curry soups, for example, benefit from a soothing Cucumber Yogurt Raita, an Indian condiment. Spicy gumbos, stews, and chiles are enhanced with savory breads such as Quintessential Cornbread and Chipotle Cornbread. Foccacia, a chewy Italian flat bread, accompanies almost any soup with panache, especially Hearty Vegetable Panade and *Soupe au Pistou.*

For a last-minute burst of flavor, Herb Forest Pesto or Poblano Rouille can be swirled into soups for instant reinvigoration and vibrancy. Soup meals served as a light lunch can be served with sweet breads and muffins such as Banana Blueberry Muffins, Yellow Squash Muffins, Herbal Biscuits, and Pumpkin Currant Scones. The recipes in this chapter bring verve and flair to the soup table.

Poblano Rouille

Rouille is a piquant Provençal sauce with an aioli-like consistency. Swirled into the soup at the finish, it provides a burst of garlicky, peppery flavor. This version exudes the mellifluous heat of poblano chiles.

1	(2-inch) slice of thick French or Italian bread, crusts removed
2	poblano chiles, roasted, peeled, seeded, and chopped
1/4	to 1/3 cup olive oil
2	cloves garlic, minced
1/4	teaspoon salt

Soak the bread in warm water for about 5 seconds. Drain, and gently squeeze out the excess water (like a sponge). In a blender or food processor fitted with a steel blade, combine the bread, chiles, oil, garlic, and salt, and blend for about 5 seconds until smooth.

Transfer the paste to a storage container and refrigerate. Serve with mild brothy soups, chowders, and tomato soups in need of a flavor infusion.

Yield: 6 to 8 servings

Soup Tips

For information on roasting chiles, see page (17). If poblano chiles are not available, try substituting New Mexico chiles. You may also use two roasted red bell peppers, but add 1 or 2 jalapeño peppers (seeded and minced) to the paste.

Quintessential Corn Bread

This corn bread makes the ideal companion to gumbo, chowder, bean soups, chili, stews, and, come to think of it, almost any hearty soup meal.

1	cup yellow cornmeal
1	cup unbleached all-purpose flour
1/3	cup sugar
1	tablespoon baking powder
1/2	teaspoon salt
1	large egg plus 1 egg white, beaten
1	cup buttermilk or lowfat milk
1/4	cup canola oil
2	tablespoons chopped pimentos or roasted sweet peppers
1	cup corn kernels, fresh or frozen and thawed

Preheat the oven to 375°F.

Combine the cornmeal, flour, sugar, baking powder, and salt in a mixing bowl, and blend together. In a separate bowl, whisk together the eggs, buttermilk, oil, and pimentos. Blend in the corn. Gently fold the liquid ingredients into the dry ingredients until the mixture forms a batter.

Pour the batter into a lightly greased 8- or 9-inch round deep-dish baking pan or springform pan. Bake for 20 to 25 minutes on the middle rack until the crust is lightly browned and a toothpick inserted in the center comes out clean. Remove from the heat and let cool on a rack.

Cut into pie-shaped wedges and serve with soup.

Yield: 6 to 8 servings

Chipotle Corn Bread

While I was in Philadelphia visiting the bustling Reading Terminal Marketplace, I sampled a fabulous chipotle-laced corn bread; I couldn't wait to make it at home. It goes well with sturdy chowders, chili, and bean soups.

1	cup yellow cornmeal
1	cup unbleached all-purpose flour
1/3	cup sugar
1	tablespoon baking powder
1/2	teaspoon salt
1	large egg plus 1 egg white, beaten
1	cup buttermilk or lowfat milk
1/4	cup canola oil
1	or 2 canned chipotle peppers, seeded and minced
1	cup corn kernels, fresh or frozen and thawed

Preheat the oven to 375°F.

Combine the cornmeal, flour, sugar, baking powder, and salt in a mixing bowl, and blend together. In a separate bowl, whisk together the eggs, buttermilk, and oil. Blend in the chipotle peppers and corn. Gently fold the liquid ingredients into the dry ingredients until the mixture forms a batter.

Pour the batter into a lightly greased 8- or 9-inch round deep-dish baking pan or springform pan. Bake for 20 to 25 minutes on the middle rack until the crust is lightly browned and a toothpick inserted in the center comes out clean. Remove from the heat and let cool on a rack.

Cut into pie-shaped wedges and serve with soup.

Yield: 6 to 8 servings

Cucumber Yogurt Raita

This classic Indian condiment is a soothing balm to curry soups, spicy bisques, and bean soups. Swirl it into the bowl of soup at the table.

2   cups plain lowfat yogurt
1   cup finely chopped cucumbers (peeled if waxed)
2   or 3 tablespoons chopped fresh cilantro, mint,
     or parsley

Combine all of the ingredients in a mixing bowl. Cover and chill until ready to serve.

Yield: 6 to 8 servings

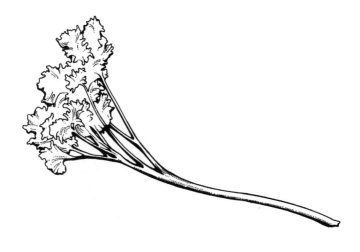

Cornbread Croutons

Sprinkle these croutons over tomato-based soups, chilies, and gumbos. Day-old cornbread makes the best croutons.

1   9-inch round cornbread (see page 239 or
     page 240)

Preheat the oven to 350°F.

Cut the cornbread into ³/4-inch cubes. Spread the cubes out on a lightly oiled baking sheet and place in the oven. Bake for 10 to 15 minutes until crusty. Remove from the oven and let cool slightly. Sprinkle the croutons over stews and soups.

Yield: 6 to 8 servings

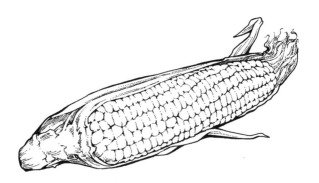

Braised Spinach Raita

This yogurt sauce brings a subtle spinach flavor to spicy soups and chilies and makes a lowfat replacement for sour cream.

2	teaspoons canola oil
2	cloves garlic, minced
1	(10-ounce) bag fresh spinach, stems removed and coarsely chopped
1/4	cup water
2	cups plain lowfat yogurt
2	tablespoons chopped fresh parsley or cilantro
1/4	teaspoon salt
1/4	teaspoon cayenne pepper

In a medium saucepan heat the oil. Add the garlic and sauté for 1 to 2 minutes. Stir in the spinach and water and cook for 3 or 4 minutes more over medium heat until wilted, stirring frequently. Remove from the heat and let cool slightly.

Drain the spinach in a colander and gently squeeze out the excess liquid. Refrigerate for 1 hour.

In a small mixing bowl combine the spinach with the yogurt and seasonings. Serve immediately, or cover and refrigerate for later.

Spoon the raita over chili or tomato-based soups, curry soups, or bean soups.

Yield: 6 servings

Herbed Whole Grain Croutons

These fat-free croutons make a crunchy topping for tomato-based soups, chowders, and chili.

  6   to 8 slices firm-textured whole grain bread,
        preferably day old
  2   tablespoons mixture of dried oregano, parsley,
        basil, and thyme
1/2   teaspoon red pepper flakes

Preheat the oven to 350°F.

Cut the crusts off the bread slices. Slice the bread into 1/2-inch cubes. Toss with the herbs and red pepper flakes. Place the cubes on a sheet pan lined with wax paper and bake for about 10 minutes until lightly toasted. Remove from the oven and let cool to room temperature. Store in an airtight container until ready to serve.

Yield: 6 servings

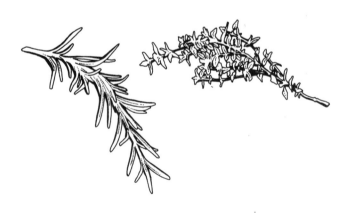

Garlic Croutons

These easy homemade croutons are a great way to use up leftover bread and add substance and flavor to a variety of soup meals in the process. Besides you can never have too much garlic on the menu.

> 6 to 8 slices firm-textured whole grain bread, preferably day old
> 2 tablespoons olive oil
> 3 or 4 cloves garlic, whole

Cut the crusts off of the bread slices. Slice the bread into 1/2-inch cubes.

In a large skillet heat the oil. Add the garlic and sauté for 3 or 4 minutes. Add the bread cubes and cook over medium heat for 5 to 10 minutes until the cubes are lightly toasted. Remove the cubes from the skillet as they become done and place on a plate lined with paper towels.

Store in an airtight container until ready to serve.

Yield: 4 to 6 servings

Yellow Squash Muffins

Yellow crookneck squash do not enjoy the kind of attention paid to their summer squash cousin, green zucchini. Yellow squash are seedier and tougher than zucchini, but the two are interchangeable in most recipes. Here they are instrumental in making these muffins moist and flavorful. These muffin treats make a great companion to almost any soup or stew.

1/2	cup canola oil
1/2	cup orange juice
1	cup brown sugar
1	large egg plus 1 large egg white, beaten
1	teaspoon vanilla extract
2	cups unbleached all-purpose flour
1	tablespoon baking powder
1	cup diced walnuts or pecans
1	teaspoon salt
1	teaspoon ground cinnamon
1	teaspoon ground nutmeg
2	cups grated yellow squash or green zucchini

Preheat the oven to 350°F.

Whisk together the oil, juice, and sugar in a mixing bowl. Add the eggs and vanilla, and continue whisking until the batter is light and creamy. In a separate bowl, combine the dry ingredients. Fold the dry mixture into the liquid ingredients, forming a batter. Gently fold in the squash.

Pour the batter into greased muffin tins and bake for 25 to 30 minutes until a toothpick inserted in the center comes out clean. Remove from the heat and let cool for a few minutes. Serve warm.

Yield: 6 large muffins or 10 to 12 medium muffins

Soup Tips

To make Squash-Carrot Muffins, substitute 1 cup shredded carrots for 1 cup of the yellow squash.

Herb Forest Pesto

I am fond of referring to my modest herb patch as a forest. Many of the poignantly flavored herbs find their way into pesto. The fragrant paste can be swirled into a variety of soups, stews, and chowders (especially tomato-based soups) for a last-minute barrage of flavor.

4	to 6 cloves garlic
1/4	cup pine nuts, walnuts, or unsalted cashews
2	juicy plum tomatoes, diced
1	cup packed fresh basil leaves
1	cup packed mixture of arugula, oregano, and mint
1/3	cup olive oil
1/2	teaspoon salt
1/2	teaspoon ground black pepper
1/3	cup grated Parmesan cheese

Place the garlic and nuts in a blender or food processor fitted with a steel blade. Process for 10 seconds, stopping once to scrape the sides. Add the tomatoes, basil, mixed herbs, oil, and seasonings, and process for 10 to 15 seconds more, until smooth. Stop at least once to scrape the sides. Transfer to a mixing bowl and fold in the cheese. Refrigerate until ready to use.

Swirl into soups at the table for a last-second surge of flavor.

Yield: About 1 1/2 cups

Skillet Roti Bread

Roti (pronounced row-tee) is a Caribbean flat bread often stuffed with a curried filling. Like pita or flour tortillas, it also accompanies soups and stews. My homemade version is slightly more biscuitlike and thicker than authentic roti, but it makes a wonderfully suitable soup companion.

4	cups unbleached all-purpose flour
2	teaspoons baking powder
1	teaspoon salt
1	teaspoon paprika
1/2	teaspoon ground cumin
1/4	teaspoon cayenne pepper
1/4	teaspoon turmeric
4	tablespoons canola oil
1	cup plus 2 or 3 tablespoons water (to mix)

Combine the dry ingredients in a mixing bowl. Gradually add the oil and water to the bowl, mixing and kneading the dough as you go. (Wet your hands if the dough is too dry.) Form a large ball with an elastic texture. Cover the dough with wax paper and set aside for 30 minutes to 1 hour.

Divide the dough into 6 equal-sized balls. On a waxed or floured surface, flatten each ball and roll out into thin 8-inch rounds or squares. Heat a lightly greased skillet over medium heat and place a roti in the pan. Cook for 4 to 5 minutes until the crust is golden brown. Flip the roti with a spatula and continue cooking until golden brown. Repeat the process with the remaining rotis.

Serve the roti bread with curry soups, bean soups, and Caribbean and Indian soups.

Yield: 6 servings

Sweet Potato Dumplings

Dumplings add both substance and flavor to soups, especially brothy vegetable soups. These chewy dumplings can be made two or three days ahead of time and added to the soup at your convenience.

2	cups peeled and diced sweet potatoes
1	cup all-purpose flour
1	large egg, beaten
2	tablespoons chopped fresh parsley (or 1 tablespoon dried parsley)
1/2	teaspoon salt

Place the sweet potatoes in boiling water to cover and cook over medium-high heat for about 15 minutes until tender, stirring occasionally. Drain the potatoes in a colander and cool slightly under cold running water. With a potato masher (or large fork), mash the potatoes in a mixing bowl.

In a medium mixing bowl combine flour, egg, parsley, and salt. Blend in the mashed potatoes to form a moist ball. With your hands form about 8 to 10 round dumplings.

To cook the dumplings, bring 6 to 8 cups of water to a boil in a large saucepan. Gently drop the dumplings one at a time into the boiling water, and cook for about 15 minutes over medium heat, stirring occasionally. Drain the dumplings in a colander.

The dumplings can now be added to a simmering soup or refrigerated for later. (If refrigerated the dumplings will keep for 2 to 3 days). After dropping the dumplings into the soup, cook for 5 to 10 minutes more over low heat.

Yield: 4 to 6 servings

Vegetarian Soup Cuisine

Bronzed Onions

When onions are sautéed until golden brown, a caramelized essence is released. Wilted browned onions are traditionally stirred into Moroccan and Middle Eastern soups and stews, especially lentil and bean pots.

1   tablespoon olive oil
1   large yellow onion, thinly slivered

In a large skillet heat the oil. Add the slivered onion and sauté for 5 to 7 minutes, until lightly browned. Remove the skillet from the heat and let cool slightly.

Serve the onions over lentil soups, Middle Eastern soups, and Lemony Lentil Soup with Bulgur Dumplings (page 200).

Yield: 4 to 6 servings

Jicama Tomato Salsa

Salsa is not just for chips. This raw salsa makes a healthful topping for chili and bean soups. Jicama, a tan-skinned tuber with a crisp texture and flavor similar to a water chestnut, gives it a nice crunch.

4	ripe tomatoes, diced
1/2	cup chopped red onion
1	red bell pepper, seeded and diced
1/2	cup peeled and diced jicama
1	jalapeño or serrano chile, seeded and minced
2	tablespoons chopped fresh cilantro
	Juice of 1 lime

In a medium mixing bowl combine all of the ingredients. Refrigerate for at least 1 hour before serving. Serve as a topping for chili and hearty bean soups.

Yield: 6 to 8 servings

Soup Tips

To prepare a jicama, peel it like a potato and dice or shred; it is most often eaten raw. Look for jicama in Latin American markets and well-stocked grocery stores.

Mint Coconut Chutney

This fragrant, nutty Indian condiment makes a cooling counterpart to spicy soups, stews, and curried broths.

1	cup shredded coconut (preferably unsweetened)
2	or 3 tablespoons chopped fresh mint leaves
2	teaspoons minced fresh ginger
1/2	teaspoon paprika
1/8	teaspoon ground cayenne pepper
1/2	cup plain lowfat yogurt
1	teaspoon fresh lemon juice

Combine all of the ingredients in a mixing bowl and blend well. Transfer to a bowl and chill for 1 hour before serving to allow the flavors to mingle.

Yield: 4 to 6 servings

Pumpkin Currant Scones

Scones can be much more than simple tea biscuits. This inventive variation makes a delightful soup companion.

2 1/2 cups all-purpose unbleached flour
2 1/2 teaspoons baking powder
1   teaspoon cinnamon
1/2 teaspoon ground nutmeg
1/2 teaspoon salt
1/4 cup brown sugar
1/4 cup margarine or butter, softened
1   (16-ounce) can pumpkin puree
1   cup whole or lowfat milk
1/2 cup currants

Preheat the oven to 400°F. Lightly grease two baking sheets.
In a medium mixing bowl combine the flour, baking powder, spices, salt, and brown sugar. Cut in the margarine or butter until the dough resembles coarse meal. With a large mixing spoon, blend in the pumpkin and milk; mix until fully incorporated. Fold in the currants and nuts.

Drop or scoop about 2 tablespoons of batter at a time onto the baking sheets, forming round balls. Scoop all of the batter onto the pans. Place in the oven and bake for 12 to 14 minutes, until the scones are lightly browned.

Let the scones cool to room temperature. Serve with soups, stews, or chilis.

Yield: 24 small scones

Banana Blueberry Muffins

Long before muffins became trendy, I was already in deep and deeply addicted. To give you an idea, at one point the theme of my old café was "Home of Muffin-mania." A good warm muffin is, indeed, one of life's finer pleasures. Serve these muffins as a light and tasty rejoinder to almost any soup meal.

1/2	cup canola oil
1	cup buttermilk, lowfat milk, or rice milk
1	cup brown sugar
2	large eggs
2	cups mashed bananas (about 4 ripe bananas)
1 1/2 to 2 cups blueberries	
2	cups unbleached all-purpose flour
1/2	cup rolled oatmeal
2	teaspoons baking powder
1	teaspoon ground cinnamon
1	teaspoon ground nutmeg
1/2	teaspoon salt

Preheat the oven to 375°F.

Whisk together the oil, buttermilk, sugar, and eggs in a mixing bowl until the batter is light and creamy. Blend in the mashed bananas and blueberries.

In a separate bowl mix the dry ingredients. Gently fold the dry ingredients into the banana mixture, and beat until completely incorporated. Spoon the batter into lightly greased muffin tins (or paper muffin cups) and bake for 40 to 50 minutes until a toothpick inserted in the center comes out clean. Remove from the oven and let stand for about 15 minutes on a rack before serving.

Yield: About 10 large muffins

Soup Garnishes and Accompaniments   255

Focaccia

Focaccia is a flat, round Italian bread with a thick, chewy crust. It is a sophisticated, high-society pizza; however, in lieu of sauce and cheese, focaccia often includes eclectic toppings such as roasted peppers, sun-dried tomatoes, olives, and garlic, and always drizzled olive oil. Focaccia makes a delightful soup companion.

Dough:
1³/₄ cups	hot tap water (110–115°F.)
1	teaspoon active dry yeast
4¹/₄ cups	unbleached all-purpose flour
¹/₃ cup	olive oil
2	teaspoons salt

Topping:
¹/₂ cup	sun-dried tomatoes (air packed)
3	tablespoons olive oil
2	cloves garlic, minced
1	tablespoon mixture of chopped, fresh herbs (including basil, rosemary, thyme, and oregano)
¹/₂	teaspoon ground black pepper
¹/₂	teaspoon salt

In a large mixing bowl combine the water and yeast. Let stand for about 10 minutes until foamy. Whisk the liquid until the yeast is completely dissolved.

Gradually mix in the flour, oil, and salt to form a moist, soft dough. Knead the dough with your hands (or in a mixer fitted with a dough hook) for about 10 minutes. Form a large ball and place in a lightly oiled mixing bowl. Coat the dough with the oil by rolling it around in the bowl. Cover the dough with plastic wrap and allow to rise for 2 to 3 hours until doubled in bulk.

Punch down the dough and knead it until it is elastic. Form a large ball and return to the oiled mixing bowl. Cover with the plastic wrap and let rise a second time for 2 to 3 hours until doubled.

Meanwhile, make the topping. Soak the sun-dried tomatoes in warm water to cover for about 1 hour. Drain, discard the liquid, and coarsely chop the tomatoes. In a medium mixing bowl combine the tomatoes, 2 tablespoons oil, garlic, herbs, and seasonings. Set aside until the focaccia is ready to be baked.

Preheat the oven to 400°F. Lightly dust a large baking sheet with cornmeal or line it with parchment paper.

With floured hands, divide the dough into baseball-sized balls. Flatten each ball into a round shape and arrange on the baking sheet. Using a spoon, press about 1 tablespoon of topping into the center of each round. With the back of the spoon "brush" the sides of the rounds with the remaining 1 tablespoon of olive oil. Place the pans in the oven and bake for 20 minutes until the focaccias are lightly browned on bottom.

Remove the baking sheet from the oven and allow to cool on a rack.

Yield: 8 focaccias

Herbal Biscuits

These flavorful, herb-scented biscuits are a welcome companion to almost any soup or stew; they may even steal the show.

2	cups unbleached all-purpose flour
2¹/₂	teaspoons baking powder
1	teaspoon salt
¹/₄	cup margarine or butter
1	cup milk
¹/₄	cup mixture of chopped fresh herbs (such as basil, parsley, oregano, and chives)

Preheat the oven to 400°F. Lightly grease a large baking sheet.

In a medium mixing bowl combine the flour, baking powder, and salt. With a pastry cutter or your fingers, blend the margarine or butter into the flour mixture until the texture resembles a coarse meal. Blend the milk into the flour, forming a moist dough. Gently knead the dough for about 30 seconds. (If the dough is too sticky, sprinkle in a little flour). Blend in the herbs.

With a spoon or melon-ball scooper that holds about 2 tablespoons, scoop the dough onto the baking sheet. Gently press the dough into round balls; leave 2 to 3 inches between each drop. Scoop all of the batter onto the sheet. Place the sheet in the oven and bake for about 12 minutes or until the crusts are light brown.

Remove from the heat and let cool to room temperature. Store in an airtight container until ready to serve.

Yield: 10 biscuits

Vegetarian Soup Cuisine

Index

Index 263

Index 265

Index

266

About the Author

Jay Solomon has been cooking and writing about for most of his adult life. He is a chef, teacher, and cookbook author living in Ithaca, New York where for many years he owned Jay's Cafe, a restaurant featuring Caribbean and Pacific Rim cuisine. He previously owned a successful cafe and wholesale chocolate chip cookie business.

Jay teaches epicurean cooking classes throughout the country and appears frequently on *Alive and Wellness,* an alternative health show on the America's Talking cable network. His articles have appeared in a variety of magazines and newspapers.

Lean Bean Cuisine

Jay Solomon has liberated beans from the antiquated dishes of the past and transformed them into exciting and adventurous vegetarian meals. Today's bean cuisine is healthful, lean, and sophisticated. The humble legume inspires a delicious array of nouveau soups, salads, entrées, and side dishes such as Native American Posole, Cajun Gumbo with Black-Eyed Peas, and Indian Dal.

Vegetarian Rice Cuisine

The innovative and meatless recipes within this book are based on the culinary traditions of Mexico, Jamaica, Korea, Italy, Brazil, India, Greece, the Middle East, Africa, and many other locations—providing savory soups, rousing salads, enticing entrées, dramatic sauces, and delightful desserts. Recipes include: Wild Rice and Basmati Pilaf; Summer Grill Risotto; and Mango Sticky Rice.

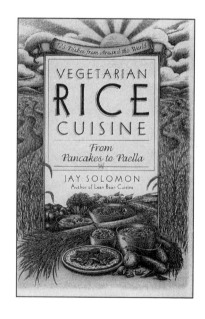

FILL IN AND MAIL TODAY

PRIMA PUBLISHING
P.O. Box 1260BK
Rocklin, CA 95677

USE YOUR VISA/MC AND ORDER BY PHONE
(916) 632-4400
Monday–Friday 9 A.M.–4 P.M. PST

I'd like to order copies of the following titles:

Quantity	Title	Amount
_____	*Lean Bean Cuisine* $12.95	_____
_____	*Vegetarian Rice Cuisine* $14.95	_____
	Subtotal	_____
	Postage & Handling ($3 for first book, $1 for additional books)	_____
	7.25% Sales Tax (California only)	_____
	TOTAL (U.S. funds only)	_____

Check enclosed for $_____ (payable to Prima Publishing)

Charge my   ❑ MasterCard   ❑ Visa

Account No. _____   Exp. Date _____

Signature _____

Your Name _____

Address _____

City/State/Zip _____

Daytime Telephone (___) _____